Praise for *Resistant*

"Dr. Abel shows us how to identify the same, repetitive spiral of interactions that drives the distressing symptoms of our anxious clients. She provides a useful decision tree of interventions for both GAD and panic to keep treatment focused. Then, within that simple structure, Dr. Abel gifts us with 86 practical strategies to help us move our clients from coping to thriving."

—Reid Wilson, PhD. Author,
Don't Panic: Taking Control of Anxiety Attacks

"This detailed, well-written guide provides practical, step-by-step instructions in a wide range of evidence-based strategies, including cognitive approaches, exposure, relaxation, and acceptance-based treatments. In addition, unlike most other books on treating anxiety, this book includes helpful chapters on treating associated problems, such as perfectionism, procrastination, and health anxiety. Dr. Abel provides an excellent roadmap for the treatment of anxiety, worry, and panic, for both novice therapists and seasoned clinicians."

—Martin M. Antony, PhD, ABPP, Author,
Anti-Anxiety Workbook

"In this concise guide to treating panic and worry, Jennifer Abel gives her innovative ideas for handling familiar techniques to every therapist who treats clients with anxiety. Her concepts of early identification of the anxiety spiral, handling exposure, using interoceptive exposure and especially her handling of familiar techniques like breathing, relaxation and in vivo exposure demonstrate her impressive practical experience that is well-founded in research. Highlighting pitfalls and obstacles to utilizing these methods, Abel takes us through the recovery process with optimism that we can help people with even the most resistant forms of anxiety."

—Margaret Wehrenberg Psy.D. author of
The 10 Best-Ever Anxiety Treatment Techniques,
The Anxious Brain, and *The 10 Best-Ever*
Depression Management Techniques

"This resource is an outstanding text for training mental health clinicians on anxiety treatment. Dr. Abel presents these strategies with substantial in-depth case examples. Dissemination of treatment research remains an issue in the treatment of anxiety disorders and this book represents a comprehensive road map to tackling treatment resistant issues. This text is an excellent contribution, useful for early career cognitive-behavioral therapists and experienced clinicians alike."

—Dr. Daniel van Ingen, author of
Anxiety Disorders Made Simple: Treatment
Approaches to Overcome Fear and Build Resiliency

"It is always a pleasure to read about Cognitive Behavioral Therapy and Exposure and Response Prevention (ERP). Rarely will an anxiety book mention the use of ERP, the most effective treatment available for anxiety. Dr. Abel presents an excellent overview of ERP and shows the reader how it can be both useful and used in daily life. Utilizing ERP, along with the other principles outlined in this book, therapists and consumers will be able to work toward reducing anxiety in empirically validated ways for maximum effect."

—Patrick B. McGrath, Ph.D., Director,
Alexian Brothers Center for Anxiety and
Obsessive Compulsive Disorders

Resistant Anxiety, Worry, and Panic

86 Practical Treatment Strategies for Clinicians

JENNIFER L. ABEL, PH.D.

PESI
Publishing
& Media
www.pesipublishing.com

Published by
PESI Publishing & Media
PESI, Inc
3839 White Ave
Eau Claire, WI 54703

Printed in the United States of America

ISBN: 978-1-937661-23-6

Cover Design: Documation
Editor: Marietta Whittlesey
Copy editor: Kayla Huset
Page Design: Bookmasters

PESI
Publishing
& Media
www.pesipublishing.com

Table of Contents

Panic and worry occur in spirals of interactions among thoughts, images, physiological sensations, behaviors and emotions, including anxiety. Learn the similarities and differences between worry and panic spirals.

Section One: Traditional and New Pragmatic Approaches to Coping Strategies

As in medicine, finding ways both to catch anxiety early and prevent the spirals from ever starting are key in the treatment of worry and panic. Learn how to teach clients to maintain relaxation throughout the day, intervene early and the research that supports the utility of these methods.

Self-Control Desensitization is a technique that provides clients with multiple repetitions of catching anxiety early in the session, thereby weakening their anxious habits and strengthening new, more relaxed habits.

Research indicates that trying to not worry actually exacerbates it and interferes with problem solving. To remedy, teach clients to: 1) move toward relaxation rather than away from anxiety; 2) use process words instead of commands; 3) postpone worry; and 4) use problem solving in favor of worry.

Simply observing one's thoughts, physical sensations, and emotions often relieves anxiety. Using various metaphors, such as the Chinese Finger Trap and Devil's Snare can help clients to accept anxiety, thereby relieving it. When observation and acceptance aren't effective, learn the trick of labeling to melt it away.

In this chapter, learn several creative new relaxation strategies, as well as traditional ones.

Traditional cognitive therapy is too complex or often too positive to the point of not being useful because it's not believed. Dr. Abel's simple strategy of using "better but believable" thoughts, or B³s, makes cognitive therapy easy to use and therefore more effective.

Anxious people often add to their feelings of pressure with the frequent use of imperatives by telling themselves that they "should" or "need to" act in a certain way. Finding "the want" in every situation eases tension and improves motivation. Also learn strategies to combat superstitious worry, as well as the use of humor, the Socratic method, and the worry prediction log.

Section Two: Negative Reinforcement and Exposure Therapies

In an effort to find relief, clients who suffer from panic attacks avoid or escape anxiety in a way that provides temporary relief only to exacerbate their anxiety in the long run. Learn to assess for the various ways in which clients negatively reinforce their anxiety and be able to teach clients to understand and change these habits.

Learn to help your clients systematically face fearful situations that cause anxiety, whether live or by guiding them through imagining themselves in these situations. These methods help clients to habituate and desensitize, alleviating their fears.

Clients who suffer from panic usually fear physiological symptoms; interoceptive exposure involves systematic exercises that trigger these symptoms repeatedly until the client gets comfortable with them. Similarly, flooding feared thoughts and words, and the use of technology can all help clients overcome their fears.

Section Three: Common Characteristics of Clients with GAD and Panic and How to Treat Them

Perfectionism not only causes a great deal of tension, it can interfere with the treatment of both panic and worry. Dispel the myth that breaks waste time, that success is the opposite of failure, and that high stress leads to high productivity. Then help clients change these negatively reinforcing behaviors.

Many people have anxiety because they are too busy taking care of others' needs that they don't take care of themselves and end up overwhelmed. Help clients to continue to help others because they "want to" and stop negatively reinforcing their habits to help out of guilt and fear.

For those whom procrastination leads to greater productivity and creativity without significant consequences, I recommend "planned procrastination" that eliminates guilt and worry associated with procrastination. For others, using small scheduled goals is more helpful.

Worry about getting sick can lead to panic, and panic attacks can often trigger hypochondriasis. Help clients to stop negatively reinforcing these fears by resisting their urges to surf the internet, seek reassurance, and check their vitals. Using interoceptive exposure and flooding their disease and death fears are also key in alleviating hypochondriasis.

While CBT is generally very effective in the treatment of worry and panic, some clients' responses to therapy are disappointing. This section presents alternative treatment approaches.

About this Book

The inspiration for this book stemmed from regularly seeing clients who had seen multiple therapists for their anxiety with little or no relief. Many of them had been to therapists who professed to practice cognitive behavioral therapy, known to be the most effective approach in treating all of the anxiety disorders. Most of these previously treatment-resistant clients have responded very well to my therapeutic approach, finally finding relief after suffering for years and sometimes decades. I attribute this success to my specialized training in anxiety with some of the top experts in worry and panic, as well as my commitment to the scientist-practitioner model, creativity, and decades of clinical experience. My specialization in anxiety disorders began with a practicum in anxiety in graduate school in 1989 and continued with training with some of the top experts in the field of panic (Georg Eifert) and worry (Tom Borkovec).

Unlike academicians who write books like this, I have committed over 20 years to a full time private practice seeing almost exclusively clients with anxiety disorders. Nonetheless, I have a solid background in research and continue to attend conferences and study the literature to keep abreast of the latest findings. My pragmatic approach to psychotherapy has led me to integrate these findings with creative solutions when clients have been stuck and then continue to use these strategies effectively with others. Therefore you will learn treatment strategies that come directly from the research literature on worry, anxiety, and panic, as well as useful strategies from my own practice that you will not learn about anywhere else.

Introduction to Worry and Panic: Characteristics of Anxiety Spirals

Whether it is fueled by worry or panic, anxiety occurs in a spiral of interactions among thoughts, images, physical sensations, behaviors, and emotions that begin insidiously and spiral out of control. Not everyone experiences all five aspects of the spiral, but thoughts, physical sensations, and the emotion of anxiety are almost always a part. For each individual, the spiral runs a similar course, or pattern, each time. Some experience only anxiety, however, the emotions of frustration, anger, and hopelessness or helplessness are also frequently present. Similarly, prolonged anxiety can often lead to depression or dysthymia.

For clients with generalized anxiety disorder (GAD), the worry spiral typically begins with a thought and spirals over the course of several minutes and sometimes several hours. Stressors of the day often fuel the spiral. The individual may not even be aware that he or she is worrying until the spiral is out of control. Similar to the fact that we can all distract ourselves from mild to moderate pain, but not from severe pain, the worried person may not notice anxiety until it becomes uncomfortable (e.g., nausea develops) or begins to interfere with functioning (e.g., difficulty concentrating). At this point, attempts to alleviate anxiety are often useless and may actually serve to fuel the spiral. This fueling may occur from the energy spent *trying* to relax, thereby causing or increasing tension. Frustration and hopelessness may be heightened when attempts to alleviate anxiety are unsuccessful–often leading to even higher levels of anxious thoughts, behaviors, physical sensations, images, or other emotions.

Although the *Diagnostic and Statistical Manual of Mental Disorders-5* (*DSM-5™*) (American Psychiatric Association, 2013) doesn't specifically mention an anxiety spiral, the symptoms that appear in the diagnostic criteria for

GAD that are often part of that spiral are: uncontrollable worry, difficulty concentrating, irritability, feeling keyed up and on edge, muscle tension, insomnia, and difficulty relaxing. We examined 40 clients with GAD (Abel & Borkovec, 1995) and compared their responses to those of 38 non-anxious control subjects utilizing the ADIS-R (Anxiety Disorders Interview Schedule-Revised; Di Nardo & Barlow, 1988) to examine the incidence of symptoms. We found an exaggerated startle response to be much more common among individuals with GAD (70%) as compared to non-anxious controls (2.8%). More troubling, gastrointestinal symptoms, including nausea, diarrhea, and vomiting, were reported by 72.5% of clients with GAD as compared to only 19.5% of subjects without GAD (Abel & Borkovec, 1995). Similarly GAD was found to be five-times more common among individuals with irritable bowel syndrome (Lee et al., 2009). Likewise irritable bowel syndrome was 4.7-times more common among individuals with GAD (Lee et al., 2009).

Panic attacks may have a gradual or rapid onset and may feel as though they come completely out-of-the-blue without warning and when least expected (e.g., from restful sleep or sitting on the couch watching TV). Yet, even when panic attacks are experienced as coming "out-of-the-blue," there is usually an insidious spiral in progress unconsciously well before it is experienced by the sufferer. Using 24-hour ambulatory monitoring with a panic button attached that collected physiological data on 43 individuals with panic disorder, Alicia Meuret and her colleagues (Meuret, et al., 2011) found that changes in heart rate, respiration, and carbon dioxide occurred an hour or more before clients reported the onset of the panic attacks. These panic attacks were reported by the clients as occurring out-of-the-blue. Surprisingly, they found very little additional physiological instability after the panic buttons were pushed, indicating that the majority of the spiral occurred before the subjects became aware of the symptoms.

A series of events may also cause the individual to feel overwhelmed, with many stressors leading to a sudden cascade of symptoms. In other cases, the panic attack begins with worry and spirals as the client "works their way into a panic." A classic panic attack peaks quickly, and the peak lasts for 10 minutes or less. Panic attacks may also occur rapidly in response to a feared stimulus (e.g., public speaking or seeing a spider for one who is phobic of them), or a stressful event (e.g., argument, being stuck in traffic). Panic attacks per se are not a diagnosable mental disorder. Clients may have a panic attack in response to an anxiety disorder, any other mental health disorder, or a medical condition. If an individual is experiencing panic attacks in response to one of these conditions and does not meet criteria for panic disorder, a "panic attack specifier" is indicated after the diagnosable condition (*DSM-V*; American Psychiatric Association, 2013). This is coded after the other condition by adding "with panic attacks." So, for instance, an individual with social anxiety disorder who experiences panic attacks exclusively in social situations would be coded as: social anxiety disorder, with panic attacks.

Regardless of whether the spiral is experienced as occurring rapidly, as with sudden panic attacks, or slowly, as in worry, the course is similar each time for each individual. Each time this course is repeated, it is strengthened in memory, becoming a stronger and stronger habit. The spirals become automatic and the person who is worrying or panicked feels more anxious over time, such that there are several short spirals within one long spiral. That is to say that in a given panic attack or episode of worry there is a relatively short-lived spiral. Over the course of time, however, these spirals become progressively more habitual, more frequent, and more severe such that over the course of days, weeks, and months a long-term spiral occurs. With worry it becomes more and more habitual as the worry spiral is repeatedly "practiced in memory." In panic, it occurs due to increasing "fear of fear" caused by avoidance behaviors that negatively reinforce anxiety (See Chapter 7).

Worry can also spiral into panic; both worry and, particularly, panic can lead to depression or dysthymia. In fact, a review of several studies (Brown, Barlow, & Liebowitz, 1994) reported that GAD has an earlier onset, typically prior to age 20, than depressive disorders and other anxiety disorders. They further reported that comorbidity of these disorders with GAD is high, ranging from 50 to 82% with the highest being simple phobia, social phobia, dysthymia, and major depression. A more recent study showed 65% of individuals with GAD met criteria for social phobia and 84% had at least one comorbid diagnosis. Given the high comorbidity rates with GAD combined with GAD's having the earliest onset, it appears that GAD creates a vulnerability from which these other anxiety and mood disorders emerge.

Our research supports this hypothesis as well as the importance of targeting GAD even when it is not the presenting problem. Of 55 clients who completed therapy, 43 (78.2%) had a comorbid anxiety disorder or dysthymia, despite the fact that we eliminated individuals who met criteria for panic disorder, major depressive disorder, and substance abuse (Borkovec, Abel & Newman, 1995). One year after treatment targeting GAD, 31 clients were considered successfully treated for GAD. These clients had a total of 35 comorbid diagnoses when entering the study and 32 (91.4%) of those diagnoses were no longer present at the one year follow-up.

One important difference between worry and panic is that nobody ever feels a *need* to panic. While worry is almost always uncomfortable, some people often feel a need to worry either to try to solve the problem or, for superstitious reasons (e.g., 'if I worry about it, it won't happen'). Similarly, while worry is uncomfortable, some people feel uncomfortable *not* worrying. The latter may give a false sense of control or worry may actually be used as a coping tool to prevent or lessen traumatic memories. For instance, it would be easier to worry about money than to recall being physically and emotionally traumatized as a child. That being said, amongst those with GAD, worry is experienced as being excessive and uncontrollable more days than not.

Unlike worry, panic is always avoided and often feared. In fact, fear of having another attack is part of the DSM-5 (American Psychiatric Association, 2013). c criteria for panic disorder. Even though someone may work his or her way into *feeling* panicked, according to the DSM-5 a panic attack is present only when there is "an abrupt surge" of anxiety that "reaches a peak within minutes." Nonetheless, the surge may arise from an already anxious state. Panic involves mostly physical sensations. In fact, in the DSM-5, 11 of the 13 symptoms are physical sensations. Two are essentially worries that are commonly experienced during the course of a panic attack, including fear of losing control or going crazy and fear of dying. However, fear of embarrassment is also very common and is often experienced when the person fears losing control or going crazy. Fear of others seeing them blush, faint, sweat, tremble, or otherwise notice symptoms of anxiety often creates a fear of embarrassment as well. The following is a list of the DSM-5 symptoms of a panic attack:

1. *Palpitations, pounding heart, or accelerated heart rate*
2. *Sweating*
3. *Trembling or shaking*
4. *Sensations of shortness of breath or smothering*
5. *Feeling of choking*
6. *Chest pain or discomfort*
7. *Nausea or abdominal distress*
8. *Feeling dizzy, unsteady, lightheaded, or faint*
9. *Chills or heat sensations*
10. *Paresthesias (numbness or tingling sensations)*
11. *Derealization (feeling of unreality) or depersonalization (feeling of being detached from oneself)*

12. *Fear of losing control or going crazy*

13. *Fear of dying*

By the time individuals suffering from anxiety come to therapy, their long-term spirals are well underway. Therefore, the focus is on treating the short-term spirals (See Chapter 1). Once the individual is doing well, then it is good to address prevention of the long-term spirals. This includes using the client and their loved one's memories of the early signs of the spirals. Once established you can develop a plan to catch these signs early the next time and utilize the coping strategies they have learned in therapy to prevent them from getting out of control.

A WORRY SPIRAL

David is driving a couple of hours to give a presentation for work the next day. He has already over-prepared for this presentation, but is worried that the delivery won't be good. He had been distracted from the presentation during work, but on the drive home he starts to think about his talk and question whether it's good enough. He begins to feel tension in the back of his neck as he imagines people falling asleep in the presentation. He grips the steering wheel tighter in an effort to feel more in control, but it only heightens his anxiety. Then he thinks, "what if someone asks a question I can't answer?" which leads to a feeling of being keyed-up and on edge. Then David begins to think about all of the things he had planned on doing before he leaves tomorrow morning and starts to worry whether he will get enough sleep. With that, he visualizes himself getting to bed late, tossing and turning all night because he is fearful he won't get enough sleep. Then he imagines himself being very tired the next day. As a result the tension builds in his entire body and he worries about the consequences of not having slept well: "What if I get into an accident because I'm so tired?" and "What if I do a terrible job because I'm so tired?" As a result, David's anxiety turns to fear and he feels more keyed up, more tense, and he gets a pit in his stomach. Then he continues to worry about his drive the next day and wonders what the weather will be like. He also worries about how difficult it will be to find the place. Therefore he worries: "What if the GPS is wrong and I'm late?" By the time he gets home, he finds it difficult to concentrate on what he had hoped to accomplish before he leaves town and he gets frustrated with himself.

(Continued)

This frustration only adds to the spiral and then it takes David hours to fall asleep that night.

Although he felt tired the next day, everything went much better than he had feared. He got to his destination safely and on time and, other than some mild to moderate anxiety, his presentation went well and was well received.

While this is a fictional representation of a possible worry spiral and the outcome, Borkovec, Hazlett-Stevens, and Diaz (1999) found that worried-about outcomes amongst individuals with GAD seldom occur. For two weeks, 27 individuals with GAD completed daily diaries recording their worries, including the feared outcome. Once the event transpired they rated the actual outcome. Sixty-eight percent of the time the reality turned out better than they had feared. Furthermore, 17 clients undergoing treatment were asked to complete similar diaries, also recording how they expected they would cope with negative events if they happened. Eighty-five percent of the time things turned out better than they had feared and, when they turned out worse, 79% of the time they dealt with the outcome better than they had feared.

A PANIC SPIRAL

Jill is driving to work and starts to feel derealized while staring at a stop-light. She immediately fears that she will have a panic attack. That fear causes her heart rate to spike and unwittingly she begins to breathe more shallowly which causes her to feel light-headed. As the light turns to green and she drives forward, she quickly fears she will pass out and wreck the car. She considers pulling over, but she looks at the clock and knows she will be late to work if she pulls over. Contemplating that decision causes her to feel overwhelmed and frustrated, because she doesn't want to risk having an accident, but she doesn't want to be late. As a result her heart beats even faster, she feels flushed, and begins to sweat. She begins to hyperventilate and feels tightness in her chest. Jill pulls over, calls in to work to tell them she'll be late. Five to 10 minutes later she feels safe to drive. She still feels anxious, but at least she's no longer afraid of passing out and wrecking the car.

While most clients relate to and understand the course of their panic spirals, they have difficulty understanding why they occur in the first place. This is especially true of individuals who do not have a history of excessive anxiety and worry. "Why did *I* start having these panic attacks?" is the frequent refrain. With a little detective work you will usually be able to figure out "the why." While figuring out "why" won't cure the panic, it is often helpful for people to recognize that, contrary to their belief, the first panic attack didn't "come out of the blue." In particular, it helps to normalize panic to reduce the fear that something is physically wrong with their body.

While there is sometimes a simple explanation for a first panic attack, there are often multiple factors at play. Those factors include:

- dehydration
- low blood sugar
- being very tired
- side-effects of prescription drugs
- taking illicit drugs
- alcohol use or, more commonly, a hangover
- excessive caffeine use
- fluorescent lights
- staring
- recently having a friend or family member have a heart attack, stroke, or similar medical event
- higher than usual "background" stress

A hangover, which involves dehydration, is a common reason for a first panic attack. The Mayo Clinic lists on their website (2011) the following symptoms as possible symptoms of a hangover:

1. *Fatigue*
2. *Thirst*
3. *Headaches and muscle aches*
4. *Nausea, vomiting or stomach pain*
5. *Poor or decreased sleep*
6. *Increased sensitivity to light and sound*
7. *Dizziness or a sense of the room spinning*
8. *Rapid heartbeat*

9. *Red, bloodshot eyes*

10. *Shakiness*

11. *Decreased ability to concentrate*

12. *Mood disturbances, such as depression, anxiety and irritability*

Note that the last symptoms of a hangover include anxiety and that four of the other symptoms are also symptoms of a panic attack: nausea, dizziness, rapid heartbeat, and shakiness. Similarly The Mayo Clinic's list of symptoms for dehydration overlap with those of a panic attack: dizziness or lightheadedness, sweating, rapid heartbeat, and rapid breathing. Finally, The National Institutes of Health lists the following symptoms of hypoglycemia, which are also consistent with those of a panic attack: shaking, sweating, feeling nervous or anxious, fast or pounding heartbeat, feeling faint (MedlinePlus, 2013).

Particularly when someone is not expecting it, just one or two of these symptoms can be terrifying, despite their often being easily explained by the individual's recent behavior and circumstances. In fact, these symptoms can cause extreme fear which exacerbates the initial symptoms and creates new symptoms, such as fear of going crazy or dying. These then trigger a spiral that elicits a sympathetic nervous system response that serves to heighten anxiety. Often the individual believes that there is a medical emergency and feels compelled to go to the emergency room. Emergency rooms typically are lit with fluorescent lights which, for many individuals, cause a sense of derealization, only serving to fuel the spiral further. Unfortunately, the emergency room physician will often prescribe benzodiazepines (e.g.,Xanax, Ativan, Klonipin). While these drugs are usually effective in reducing the anxiety in the short term, they negatively reinforce it by reducing immediate symptoms, thereby actually contributing to the long-term spiral. Similarly, avoidance, checking, reassurance, and other behaviors may help to reduce anxiety in the moment, only to help maintain and even strengthen the longer-term spiral of anxiety (See Chapter 8 for more on negative reinforcement).

Catching the anxiety spiral early and nipping it in the bud is the cornerstone of treatment for worry and GAD. Panic can certainly be somewhat ameliorated early by catching anxiety early, but exposure-based treatments typically work better in treating true panic attacks. However, in some cases, exposure-based therapies are contraindicated. Therefore, I have developed a decision tree at the end of chapter 10 for helping you to design the best treatment plan for your clients who suffer from panic attacks.

SECTION ONE

Traditional and New Pragmatic Approaches to Coping Strategies

Anxiety is much easier to manage when detected early. Most cognitive behavioral strategies that are very effective when anxiety is caught early are of limited use once worry and panic have gained momentum. This section begins by highlighting the importance of preventing and intervening early in the anxiety spiral as well as explaining how to teach clients to catch the early cues of anxiety. You will learn how to do self-control desensitization; a means of strengthening the habit of catching the anxiety spiral early with repeated practice. You will also learn applied, or active, relaxation which can help to prevent spirals from occurring by keeping one relaxed throughout the day.

The remaining chapters in this section are cognitive-behavioral coping strategies, most of which are best used early in the anxiety spiral. Many of the strategies, while familiar, are presented in a way to maximize their effectiveness in the treatment of panic and GAD. While most of these strategies have a basis in traditional CBT, there are several useful new twists presented. These include, but aren't limited to, postponing worry, the use of process words in teaching relaxation, the use of metaphors in mindful acceptance, a simpler, more pragmatic approach to cognitive therapy. While the strategies presented in this section can be helpful in treating panic, their application to worry and GAD is particularly beneficial. The information and strategies presented in section two are more useful for the treatment of panic attacks.

CHAPTER ONE

Early Cue Detection and Prevention

Given that both worry and panic occur in a spiral of interactions among thoughts, images, physical sensations, and behaviors that start out insidiously and spiral out of control, it is optimal to notice and intervene in the anxiety spiral early in order to prevent it from spinning out of control. We frequently see the value of early intervention in the medical field. From cancer to Lyme disease to multiple sclerosis, and many other diseases, early detection and diagnosis optimize outcomes. However, most mental health care professionals were not trained to "catch" anxiety, depression, or other mental disorders early. Yet the old adage, "an ounce of prevention is worth a pound of cure" is very applicable to working with our clients who worry excessively or have panic attacks. There are three reasons that there is an advantage to teaching clients to detect the early symptoms of anxiety and panic, and rapidly apply coping strategies.

The first is that we can catch the anxiety when it is weakest and treatment strategies will be more powerful. The second is that each

> Strategy #1: Catch the anxiety spiral early.

time our clients catch the anxiety early, their spiral is weakened in memory. It's like putting the worries and symptoms of worry in an emotional sling, so to speak, such that the "worry muscle" atrophies. The worry habit gets weaker the longer it is prevented from being practiced in memory. Finally, each time clients apply coping strategies early in the spiral a new habit begins to emerge. The habit of catching anxiety early and applying various coping strategies becomes both easier and more automatic. So much so that in the course of therapy when you ask your clients what their anxiety level is (e.g., on a 1-10 scale) they will start to ask you "before or after you asked?" because the habit of letting-go has become so strong that merely asking what their anxiety level triggers an automatic and rapid process of easing anxiety.

Even better than catching anxiety early, is preventing the spiral from ever taking hold in the first place. So in addition to the emphasis on catching anxiety early, it is very useful to teach a habit of frequent relaxation and mindful practice throughout the day, even when clients don't feel like it is needed. For instance, if we consider an anxiety level of a "2" on a 1-10 scale to be optimal for feeling relaxed yet capable of functioning very efficiently, it is useful to employ relaxation strategies any time the client is above a "2" even if they don't consider themselves to be anxious. So, for instance, if Andrea typically fluctuates between a "4" and a "6" she may *feel* as though she doesn't need to employ her strategies when she is experiencing a "4" or a "5." But consider how Andrea might react differently when faced with a stressor if she had lowered a "4" to a "2." Perhaps she realizes that she double-booked her schedule. She told her friends she could get together with them after work on Wednesday and then realizes that she had forgotten about a work commitment that didn't make it into her calendar. If she is at that "4" when she makes this discovery she might become a "6" or a "7" after realizing it. However, if she has been utilizing skills to maintain relaxation at a "2" she will likely be more accepting of her blunder and look for a solution rather than getting riled-up about it. Her anxiety level may not rise at all or, if it does, it will likely not rise as high and she will likely recover more rapidly. Similarly, if a spiral of anxiety ensued from this discovery, she's more likely to be able to catch that spiral at a lower level and prevent it from getting out of control.

You want to encourage your clients to practice several times per day the coping strategies that you teach them. I have had clients who estimate that they are applying mindful and relaxation strategies upwards of 40 times

> **Strategy #2: Active Relaxation – frequent relaxation throughout the day.**

per day. At this point you might be thinking that this is an unrealistic goal and that it would be distressing to relax that many times a day. If you are thinking that you would ask your clients to stop, close their eyes, and take a moment to relax, then you are absolutely correct, this would be counterproductive. To the contrary, encourage your clients to continue their flow of activity, applying the strategies without stopping unless they have a few moments and wish to get more deeply relaxed.

Many therapists teach their clients to practice getting deeply relaxed by taking 10-30 minutes per day engaging in meditation or progressive muscle relaxation and stopping there. Likewise people striving for a more relaxing lifestyle learn relaxation strategies, but practice these strategies in a quiet place a few times per week for several minutes. I certainly advocate teaching deep relaxation and setting aside at least a few minutes each day to engage in these practices. However, it has been shown that teaching cognitive behavioral therapy techniques, including progressive-muscle relaxation, cognitive therapy, and mindfulness, without regard to catching the spiral early is minimally effective in treating generalized anxiety disorder (Barlow et al.,1984; Blowers, Cobb, & Mathews, 1987; Borkovec & Mathews, 1988; Borkovec et al., 1987; Butler, Fennell, Robson, & Gelder, 1991). That is, although CBT is more effective than non-directive therapy or no therapy at all, the effect sizes were disappointing and small.

Borkovec and Costello (1993) developed applied relaxation based on their recognition of the anxiety spiral and their hypothesis that teaching clients to intervene early and prevent anxiety would be more effective than traditional CBT. It involves a bit of a paradigm shift in thinking about the role of relaxation in letting go of anxiety, panic, and worry. Rather than the focus being on deep relaxation on a daily or twice-daily basis, there is an emphasis on maintaining relaxation throughout the day no matter where the individual may be or what they may be doing. Because this requires absolutely no time there is virtually no limit to the number of times or the number of hours during the day an individual can be mindful of keeping themselves relaxed by utilizing these "portable" strategies. To demonstrate this practice, begin focusing on the surfaces beneath you while continuing to read on. Becoming aware of the surfaces beneath your legs and feet while continuing to read on without it slowing the speed in which you are reading. In fact, you may want to continue to periodically focus part of your attention on these surfaces beneath you or on a relaxation strategy of your choice as you continue to read. Notice that you can keep reading at the same pace, while utilizing a relaxation strategy. Now that you understand this concept and have experienced it first-hand, you can teach this strategy, called applied relaxation, to your clients.

To test their hypothesis, Borkovec and Costello (1993) compared three groups in the treatment of GAD: non-directive therapy, applied relaxation, and self-control desensitization. Self-control desensitization (Goldfried, 1971) involves beginning with relaxation, introducing anxiety-producing stimuli, and applying relaxation at the earliest sign of anxiety. It is explained in detail in the next chapter. The results of this study were very promising in that both of the groups utilizing strategies to catch anxiety early were more effective than the non-directive group, and the findings were more robust than those of studies using CBT without the application of early anxiety detection followed by rapid application of coping strategies. Subsequent studies have continued to support early intervention and prevention (Newman, Castonguay, Borkovec, Fisher, & Nordberg, 2008). In one study fewer than 9% of clients met criteria for GAD at the end of the study and only 17% did so at two-year follow up (Borkovec, Newman, Pincus, & Lytle, 2002).

Early cue detection is also useful in preventing panic attacks. Barlow and Craske (2006) have found that learning early triggers of panic and applying a variety of coping strategies, such as cognitive therapy and diaphragmatic breathing, plays a useful role in the effective treatment of panic disorder. However, interoceptive exposure also plays a significant role in treating panic. See the decision tree at the end of Section Two to decide whether early cue detection or interoceptive exposure is indicated for each specific client suffering from panic attacks.

When teaching clients about the anxiety spiral and the utility of applying coping behaviors to prevent it from getting out of control, it is very useful to provide a rationale. Once I have determined from an assessment that an individual is a good candidate for the worry program, I briefly explain CBT. Then typically I guide him or her through some form of relaxation/meditation before I present the rationale for early cue detection by saying something similar to this:

> *In the late 80's and early 90's researchers began to use relaxation and cognitive therapy to treat generalized anxiety and worry. While it was more effective than talk therapy, the results were disappointing. Many people still suffered from anxiety and worry. Fortunately, psychologists at Penn State didn't give up. Instead they hypothesized that the strategies used in these studies could be more much more powerful if anxiety sufferers were taught the right time to use them. They realized that worry and anxiety occur in a spiral of interactions among thoughts, images, physical sensations, and behaviors that start out insidiously and spiral out of control. With this knowledge they strategize to catch these anxiety spirals early, when they are weakest, and applying relaxation and other coping strategies, thereby preventing them from getting out of control. Once they taught people who worry excessively to catch the spirals early and utilize relaxation and cognitive therapy throughout the day, the effects were much better. In fact, by the third study (Borkovec et. al, 2002) more than 91% of the participants no longer met criteria for GAD at the end of treatment and at two-year follow up 83% still enjoyed this success.*

One of the ways I teach clients to remember the importance of using the preventive strategies that I teach them early on in their spiral is to think of the three popular adages that describe the utility of prevention and early intervention: "An ounce of prevention is worth a pound of cure" for prevention and, for early detection and prevention of the beginning of a spiral from getting out of control: "a stitch in time saves nine" and "nip it in the bud."

Now I'd like to give you an example of an anxiety and worry spiral with a stay-at-home mom, who we'll call Emily:

*Emily is cooking dinner, and she isn't anxious at all. She's chopping some vegetables when she begins to spiral with a couple of thoughts: "Gee, it seems like it's getting late. I wonder what time it is?" With those thoughts she gets a little tension in the back of her neck. Emily sets down her knife and looks at the clock on the microwave and she sees that it is, in fact, a little late, which causes the tension in her neck to build and spread to her shoulders and upper back. Without really thinking about it, she automatically walks over to the window, and when she doesn't see her husband's car coming down the road, she immediately gets a knot in her stomach. If it's a beautiful day she might worry that he's having an affair. If it's cloudy or rainy, she jumps to the conclusion that he's been in an accident. At this point, her worry and anxiety turns into fear as she has a visual image of her husband's wrecked car, she hears emergency vehicles in her mind, and visualizes him in an ambulance with the paramedics working on him on the way to the hospital. Then Emily begins to pace as a way to deal with the energy from her anxiety and soon her heart is racing and pounding with fear. She soon recalls the many times that she has paced while worrying about her husband being late in the past and gets really frustrated with him. She thinks, "He knows that I worry about him and yet he does this to me all the time. It's so frustrating that he gets mad at me when I call to find out if he's okay." But then she visualizes him unconscious in a hospital bed hooked up to ventilators. At that point she is reminded that she has a problem with worry, so she tries to think more positively and tries a breathing technique she has learned. This actually makes things a little worse for Emily, because it takes energy to **try** the breathing and changing her thinking. Also, the fact that it doesn't help at this stage causes additional frustration and even hopelessness.*

Now imagine the scenario a day or two after Emily has had a session and learned the importance of early cue detection in catching anxiety early: *She is chopping the vegetables when she gets the thought: "Gee, it seems like it's getting late. I wonder what time it is?" With those thoughts she gets a little tension in the back of her neck. She sets down her knife and looks at the clock on the microwave and she sees that it is, in fact, a little late, causing the tension to build. But at the same moment she also sees a sticky-note that she has attached to the microwave near the clock. When she sees the sticky-note, it serves as a reminder to utilize coping strategies.* (While one may choose to write a word such as "calm" on the sticky-note, a blank one will also serve the purpose.) *Instead of walking to the window to see if her husband is coming, she gently shifts her attention back to chopping her vegetables. She focuses on the ground beneath her feet, the knife in her hand and the smell of the food she is cooking.*

Imagine how much easier it will be for Emily to manage a mild level of anxiety after catching the spiral early versus a high level of anxiety after the spiral has gained momentum. In the first case, Emily had only to contend with the thought "he is late" and tension in her back and neck. In the second case, she was faced with managing the thought he is late, tension in her back and neck, a pit in her stomach, racing heart, fear, irritability, frustration, images of her husband in a car wreck and hooked up to a ventilator, and worry about being able to take care of the kids without him. Any coping strategy will be far more likely to be effective when the spiral is weaker as a result of catching it early.

Given that early cue detection of the anxiety spiral is the crux of worry treatment it's very important for clients to understand and remember it. Therefore, I recommend a visual along with the verbal explanation, because it's likely that clients will process the idea better. So I enact the scenario by using my planner and bookmark, for example, and say: "Pretend I am a stay-at-home mom chopping vegetables, this is my knife (holding up the bookmark) and this planner is my cutting board." I first enact the scenario where the spiral gets out of control. Then I put a sticky note on the clock I keep in my window and enact the early detection.

Most of the time therapists teach their clients useful strategies, but don't teach them the right time to utilize them. What usually hap-

> Strategy #3: Use external reminders to stay relaxed.

pens is that clients are very much like Emily. They may not even be aware that they are spiraling until the anxiety is already out of control, and the coping strategies are useless against the more severe level of anxiety. In general, therapists aren't aware of how critical it is to catch anxiety early. Merely encouraging clients to catch anxiety early is *not* enough because the spiral usually has a great deal of momentum once the worried person becomes aware of the anxiety.

Therefore, frequent reminders are very useful in helping clients to maintain relaxation and prevent anxiety from getting out of control.

The most useful reminders to maintain relaxation and prevent anxiety from spiraling are sticky notes. They are inexpensive and can be changed frequently. Most clients find the sticky notes to be effective reminders. However, some clients find them to be anxiety-provoking or don't like them hanging around. If your client is amenable to sticky notes, suggest that they put them both in places that they associate with stress as well as places they will see frequently. So, for instance, if Emily went to the window to see if her husband was coming home before checking the clock, putting a sticky note there would be valuable even if she only looks out that window looking for her tardy husband three to four times per week. Emily may not find using the water dispenser to be at all anxiety-producing, but putting a sticky note near it is particularly useful if she gets water many times a day. Other places I suggest are:

- light switches
- doorknobs
- passageways that have no doorknobs
- pantry
- refrigerator
- clocks
- phone (land-line)
- TV remote
- TV
- computer screen
- computer keyboard
- car (both driver and passenger side if applicable)
- books or magazines they are currently reading
- notebooks
- planner
- dresser
- faucets
- toilet (across from it, near the flusher or toilet paper roll)
- keys (take off just a small sticky part)

After a couple of weeks, the sticky notes will not be noticed. Much like when you purchase something new for your home or office, you notice it immediately when you walk into the room, but eventually it blends in with everything else. Therefore, I suggest that clients change notes when they realize that they are not noticing them as much. In fact, I give them a new color every couple of weeks as I believe that the ones I give them help to serve as a reminder to change them. For clients who feel connected to you, sticky notes they receive from you may have an additional value that can add encouragement to practice techniques, potentially boosting their effectiveness.

Sticky notes can serve a dual purpose for both parents and teachers. While your client knows that the sticky notes are largely to remind them to utilize their coping strategies, they can tell the children that they are reminders for them. Teachers and parents can use the notes as a way to reinforce something they are trying to teach the children. For example, a teacher can place a few blue sticky-notes around their classroom and tell the kids that they are reminders for them to raise their hands before speaking. Similarly a father may say to his son, "Billy, the green squares are a reminder for you to pick up your toys when you are finished using them."

In addition to, or instead of, sticky notes here are a few ideas of other reminders you may suggest for clients:

- colorful hairband to put around a water bottle, phone, mug, etc.
- repeatedly reset timer on cell phone
- change wallpaper and/or screen saver
- bell, ribbon, bandana, etc. on a pet

You can also suggest that they try to remember to use the following experiences as reminders to relax:

- when you hear a phone ring
- when you see the color of your current sticky-note reminders elsewhere during the day
- when your name is called (whether it's "Mom," "Honey," or your actual name)
- when you change activities
- when you see a person who sometimes brings stress
- when you are hungry or have a craving
- when you are thirsty

Encourage clients to spend at least 5-10 minutes per day with the sole purpose of practicing relaxation or meditation. The reason is two-fold. The first is to strengthen the practice of relaxation so that it will be more effective when applying it throughout the day. The second is to get deeply relaxed in an effort to maintain that relaxation for the rest of the day.

Toward the beginning of each session, ask your client how many times each day they utilized their coping strategies for letting go of anxiety. Initially, they will often report a low number like three or four. At this point, assess why they weren't able to do more. Most of the time they have forgotten that they do not need to stop their activities to use these strategies. However, it may be that they didn't put enough reminders into place. In this case, help them to decide on at least a dozen places from the aforementioned list where they can place sticky-notes.

If they said they didn't have time to relax when they saw the sticky-notes, emphasize that the goal is to be relaxed while being active. Empathize with them about how annoying it would be to stop everything they're doing each time they see a sticky note. Then go on to explain: "Right now we can keep up our conversation; I can talk to you and you can listen, and we can both be mindful of the surfaces beneath us. We can both be letting go of any unneeded tension." Then explain that they can focus on relaxation while they drive, eat, shower, walk, and engage in their job without stopping their flow of activity. Nonetheless, let them know that if they have a little extra time it is fine to stop and get even more deeply relaxed.

You may see clients who complain that they cannot catch their anxiety early, because they are constantly anxious. In these cases, find out when they are *least* anxious. There is

> Strategy #4: Practice strengthening relaxation when least stressed.

always a time when even the most anxious individuals feel less anxious. This may be a specific time of day or it might be after a particular event. So, for instance, some people say that they are least anxious in the morning, while others say they are least anxious at night. Many people may say they are least anxious right after they exercise. Some feel least anxious after dinner, after sex, or on the weekends. Chances are, if they have ever tried to use relaxation skills, it hasn't been to try them when they are least anxious. However, that is exactly what you want to do when clients complain that they are always anxious. When you encourage them to practice relaxation when they are least stressed this is also the time they are most likely to become successfully relaxed. Then, the goal is to maintain that relaxation throughout the day.

In difficult cases, clients may continue to state that they are unable to relax and contend that catching the spiral early is of no use to them because they are *always* very anxious. Nonetheless, I have never encountered an instance in which the client is unable to identify a time that they are less anxious than others. However, sometimes they will need assistance in discovering that time. You might want to try a Socratic approach (See the Socratic Method section of Chapter 7). The following is a script of how you might approach a difficult client:

Therapist: When do you feel most relaxed?

William: I never feel relaxed. From the moment I wake up to the moment I go to bed, I'm wound up.

Therapist: Even on the weekends?

William: Yup!

Therapist: Is there a time of day you are less anxious?

William: Not really.

Therapist: Are you most relaxed on the weekends or on the weekdays?

William: Depends.

Therapist: What do you do for fun or relaxation?

William: I run.

Therapist: How do you feel during and after you run?

William: Yeah! Now that you mention it, I guess that is the time I'm most relaxed, just after I run and probably even during the run.

Therapist: Great! So the goal is going to be maintaining that relaxation after your run. How would you feel about taking a 5-10 minute walk at the end of your run?

William: I don't know. Sometimes I'm in a time crunch and don't even get as much running as I want.

Therapist: Well, maybe on the weekends? Or maybe you'll decide it will be worth it to sacrifice 5 minutes of your run to practice being in the moment.

William: That makes sense. I'll start by trying it on the weekends when I have more time.

Therapist: You can also focus on your senses while you're running. You might already be doing that now. It might be part of why you are relaxed on a run. Maybe you are already focusing on the changing landscape, the feeling of the sun and wind, the smells.

William: Probably at least part of the time, yeah.

Therapist: Perhaps you can devote at least part of your run to focusing on your senses purposefully?

William: Ok, I could do that!

Therapist: Do you usually take a shower after you run?

William: Oh yeah! Pretty much always.

Therapist: Ok! So while in the shower, focus on the sound and the feeling of the water, the smell of the shampoo and soap, see the water flowing out of your shower head. In other words, take the opportunity to be in the moment while you're showering to help you maintain the relaxed feeling you have after a run.

William: Yeah! I'm usually pretty relaxed in the shower anyway. But during the week when I get in the car I usually start worrying about all I have to do at work, and my relaxation is over.

Therapist: Great! Sounds like we've discovered a time where you feel relaxed and the time when the spiral begins to take hold. Putting a sticky note in your car will help to remind you to begin to change that habit you have of worrying on your way into work and give you an opportunity to begin to catch your worry spiral early while at the same time beginning to form a new habit—one in which you continue your relaxation on the way into work.

William: Sounds good, except I often have phone calls to make on my way in.

Therapist: Not a problem. You can make your calls while focusing on the surfaces beneath you and what you see around you as you drive—the cars in front of you and in your periphery, the sky in front of you, and other things you can notice safely. You can talk and focus on your senses at the same time, and this will help to prevent your spirals from getting out of control. As long as you're focusing on what you see, you'll probably even be a safer driver.

For individuals who have panic attacks, maintaining relaxation throughout the day can help to prevent them. This is particularly true for cases in which the anxious person gradually worries his or her way into a panic

> Strategy #5: Use the panic attack monitoring form to learn patterns in order to prevent them.

attack. For those panic attacks that feel as though they are coming out of the blue, a little detective work is useful. In either case, ask your clients to complete the panic attack monitoring form below (feel free to make copies of it). This form can be helpful in elucidating the early contributing factors to clients' panic attacks. The goal is for the unpredictable to become predictable by seeing patterns and utilizing strategies when those patterns begin to emerge. Once the triggers and early symptoms of panic attacks become clear this information can be used to prevent panic attacks from occurring.

Interoceptive exposure (See Chapter 11) is usually more effective in treating panic than catching anxiety early in cases where the anxiety seems to come out of the blue, when the threat of having additional panic attacks is feared, and when there is a fear of dying or suffering a serious medical event. Having your clients complete this monitoring form is very helpful in deciding which interoceptive exposure exercises will be most effective.

To summarize, a common pitfall of teaching meditation, relaxation, and other coping strategies designed to alleviate anxiety is teaching clients to get deeply relaxed once or twice a day without emphasizing the importance of frequent application of these strategies throughout the day to help maintain relaxation and prevent anxiety. Likewise, failing to address the nature of the anxiety spiral along with the importance of catching the spiral early and applying coping strategies is a common problem. *Relaxation and mindfulness are most useful when practiced multiple times throughout the day, without stopping the flow of activity.* The goals of frequent application of coping strategies are two-fold: 1. Maintain relaxation throughout the day no matter where or when to prevent anxiety; 2. Catch the anxiety spiral early to prevent it from getting out of control. Over time, most clients who make a reasonable effort toward this practice will find that utilizing these skills will become increasingly automatic such that they will relax with little effort and eventually bypass "internal relaxation instruction" to relax immediately. So, for instance, the sticky-note reminders will immediately lead to letting the muscles relax without thinking "soften my muscles." These practices will help to manage anxiety, worry, and panic by decreasing the frequency, intensity, and length of time clients experience anxiety.

PANIC ATTACK MONITORING FORM

Time:

Situation (where, who, what):

Background Stress (hour/s leading up to panic):

Symptoms: Check all that were experienced, circle the first, underline the worst

_____heart rate increase   _____chest pain or discomfort
_____sweating   _____derealization or depersonalization
_____trembling or shaking   _____numbness or tingling sensations
_____difficulty breathing   _____chills or hot flushes
_____feeling of choking   _____fear of losing control or going crazy
_____nausea or abdominal distress _____fear of dying
_____feeling dizzy, unsteady, or faint _____(other)_____

Intensity of Panic 0-10 _____

Worked Into Panic _____ Came Out of the Blue _____

CHAPTER TWO

Self-Control Desensitization

Self-Control Desensitization (SCD) was introduced by Marvin Goldfried (1971) and was developed by Tom Borkovec specifically to treat worry. This technique helps clients form the habit of early cue detection by practicing it in the therapy session. In brief, what I call "formal SCD" involves getting the client deeply relaxed and then presenting an anxiety-producing trigger

> Strategy #6: Formal Self-Control Desensitization: To practice catching anxiety early.

(image, thought, physical sensation). The instant the client feels less relaxed, he or she signals by raising their index finger. This is followed immediately by acceptance or relaxation (See Chapters 4 and 5). "Informal SCD" involves beginning a session with relaxation and then periodically throughout the remainder of the session presenting a reminder to utilize various anxiety reduction strategies without stopping the flow of the session.

FORMAL SCD

Before starting formal SCD, discuss with your client what they have been worried about and how it has been affecting them. Specifically ask how it has manifested in their body. Review the importance of catching anxiety early and nipping it in the bud. Follow with an explanation that a process called self-control desensitization will help them to develop this practice into a habit by repeatedly practicing catching anxiety early and letting it go. After this go on to explain the procedure by saying something like this:

> *I will guide you through relaxation. After you appear to be deeply relaxed, I will introduce things that I expect will trigger some anxiety. However, don't wait until you feel anxious. Instead, as soon as you feel a little less relaxed, I'd like for you to raise your index finger* (demonstrate by keeping your hand on your leg and lifting only your index

finger. Otherwise, some people will raise their hand and there is an advantage to exerting less effort). *Hold up your finger until you feel completely relaxed again and then lower it* (again, demonstrate your finger completely relaxing on your leg). *So, for instance, if after you get very relaxed you consider yourself to be at a "2" on a 0-10 scale, when you feel you are at a "2.1" raise your finger. In all likelihood your level will go higher than that, but the idea is to nip this spiral in the bud repeatedly. This will provide you with a great deal of practice letting go early in the spiral before your anxiety gets out of control. This practice will help you to form a habit of letting go of anxiety early. The habit you can learn is to use relaxation strategies before your anxiety has a chance to gain momentum. Okay, let your head rest against a pillow and close your eyes.*

At this point you will guide your client through relaxation (use strategies in your repertoire and see Chapters 4 and 5). Then say something like this "keeping your eyes closed, what is your anxiety level on a 1-10 scale?" You may not want to proceed with SCD until the level is below a "4." However, if your client came into the session after a spiral had already gained momentum, acceptance strategies followed by guided meditation may be helpful. If not, you may want to postpone SCD to another time. Remember, the goal of SCD is to prevent anxiety from getting out of control. If their anxiety is already high, SCD for that session is contraindicated unless you are able to get them relaxed with acceptance and coping strategies first.

Once your client is relaxed, bring up a worry (e.g., *"worry about your speech tomorrow ..."*), an image (e.g., *"visualize that you are at work and it's 5 minutes before you are to deliver your speech ..."*), or a physical sensation (e.g., *"remember how that heavy sensation in your chest feels and allow it to feel that way now ..."*). If they don't raise their finger after about 20 seconds then a gentle reminder is in order (e.g. "remember to raise your finger even if you feel slightly less relaxed"), because sometimes clients get so relaxed that they forget to raise their finger even after feeling less relaxed. Continue repeating the worry, adding increasingly anxiety-producing thoughts if the client doesn't raise their finger within about 20 sec. The moment they raise their finger either begin with acceptance patter (See Chapter 4) (patter is a series of words used in the process of acceptance or relaxation) followed by relaxation patter (See Chapter 5.). Or, if the client has not responded well to acceptance in the past, then go directly to relaxation. In the former case, as soon as your client raises their finger you might say something like this:

Observing the feeling in your chest, allowing it to be there, and gently letting go by shifting your attention to the surfaces beneath you.

Then, when they lower their finger, either repeat the same stressful words or change them. You can change to a different topic altogether or shift to a different type of stressor (e.g., move from a physical sensation to an image). When presenting an image, purposefully bring your client back to your office, back to the present, as soon as their finger is raised. Note that to help a client relax, I use process words such as "observing" or "allowing" rather than the commands "observe" or "allow." The reasons for this will be discussed in more detail in Chapter 3.

Usually you will see progress within 10-15 minutes. It is common to observe that it takes progressively more time before you observe their finger going up and a shorter period of time in which their finger stays up. When this happens you know that relaxation and/or acceptance skills are getting stronger, and the worry and anxiety are getting weaker. They are developing a habit of catching anxiety early.

Once you observe the anxiety weakening, create a challenge. Challenge can be created in at least three ways. One way is to make the worry or image more negative. Another way is to combine a physical sensation with either a worry or imagery. When using imagery, and the client has succeeded in quickly letting go, instead of "bringing them back to the office" have them continue to visualize the stressful event while continuing the relaxation. In this case, the following is an example of a script to use after they have raised their finger:

> *Continue to visualize yourself staying at your office this time. Observing your worry about your review with your boss and letting go of any tension that you don't need. Focusing on the surfaces beneath you and allowing your body to relax while continuing to visualize yourself at your office before your review.* After their finger has gone down ... *noticing that you can imagine yourself at work before your review and be relaxed at the same time. (Pause) Now letting go completely by bringing yourself back to my office.*

During SCD you will be talking one hundred percent of the time, except when you move the responsibility to your client. When you are bringing up anxiety-producing thoughts you may repeat the same scenarios or add new ideas about what you know has made your client anxious in the past.

Finally, once they are letting go easily, you can shift the responsibility to the client. When their finger goes up simply say "letting go on your own" or something similar. If they seem to have difficulty such that it's taking much longer for them to get to the baseline relaxation than it did when you guided them, it can be helpful to briefly add some guidance for letting go of the struggle. So, for instance, you could say "resisting the urge to try to push the anxiety away … instead observing the anxiety and moving gently toward relaxation on your own."

To review, the following are the steps that I suggest. You can use your own discretion and creativity to alter these steps:

1. Provide the rationale for SCD as a way to practice early cue detection and develop a new habit of catching anxiety early.

2. Explain the process.

3. Determine their anxiety level on a 0-10 scale, or other scale if you prefer.

4. Ask your client to support their head and neck against the chair, couch, or a pillow and close their eyes. Begin relaxation patter.

5. If anxiety was above a 3 before beginning relaxation, check to see if it has come down. You may continue with more relaxation to get down to at least a 4. If unable to get relaxed reschedule SCD for another time.

6. Once relaxed, introduce an anxiety-producing stimulus.

7. Once they raise their finger, begin acceptance and/or relaxation patter.

8. Once they lower their finger. Repeat steps 6-8 until number 9 occurs.

9. Once your client has either taken much longer to raise their finger after the anxiety-producing stimulus is presented OR they lower their finger rapidly, proceed to step 10.

10. Change the stimulus to either a different worry, an image of the feared situation, or a physical sensation repeating 6-9.

11. THEN, EITHER:

12. **a)** Ask your client to continue the anxiety-producing imagery while relaxing. (e.g. "Continuing to see yourself at the office with your boss and relaxing at the same time. Noticing that you can visualize this scenario while remaining relaxed.")

    b) Once their finger goes up, shift the responsibility of relaxing on them (e.g. *"letting go on your own."*)

Troubleshooting for Formal SCD

The client does not appear to be able to get anxious. It's possible the client didn't understand the directions. In this case, gently remind them to raise their finger if they are even less relaxed. Also, if they are not raising their finger look for signs that they are anxious such as a change in breathing or anxious facial expressions.

If they are not getting anxious in the very beginning it is likely that they are accepting. In these instances, which don't happen too often, go with acceptance. So, for instance, you might say: *"noticing that when you allow yourself to observe the worry, it loses its power, because you are no longer struggling and you are accepting it."* See Chapter 4 for details about acceptance.

In addition, there are some clients who are only anxious during their work week. If you see them on a Friday afternoon or on their day off during the week, it may be difficult for them to be able to worry. Similarly, sometimes when clients arrive after they have been to the gym they are very relaxed and have difficulty getting anxious. Finally, clients who take benzodiazepines or other anxiolytics will often not be able to get anxious when their medications are at peak concentration. In these cases, it is best to ask your client to come in when their medication is wearing off, skip a dose, or take half a dose. When making these suggestions, it is best to communicate with the prescriber to make sure he or she is okay with you making these suggestions to their patient. Technically, if the dose is written p.r.n. (i.e., "as needed") we can ask clients to make these changes. But it is often best to communicate with the physician, or prescribing practitioner, because at some point you want to help your client titrate off of benzodiazepines. For more information on benzodiazepenes see chapters 8 and 15)

The client is unable to get relaxed from the start. First use acceptance strategies and then relaxation strategies. If the client is still not relaxing it is probably best to postpone formal SCD to another time. You might purposefully schedule the next visit for a time where the client is more relaxed. Think the opposite of above. That is, bring them in on their day off, after their workout, on a small dose of their prescribed p.r.n. medication, if they are more relaxed at those times.

The client is unable to get relaxed once you have brought up the stressful patter. Simply be patient. There is a great deal of variability in clients' responsiveness to SCD. Some are able to relax within a few seconds, others may take a full minute or more. Also, remember to use a variety of strategies including observing and accepting the anxiety. So, for instance, if acceptance and focusing on senses is not helpful, it may be best to use imagery, muscle relaxation, or diaphragmatic breathing combined with imagery. You may also utilize cognitive therapy.

The client may have had difficulty relaxing because they waited until they got anxious to raise their finger. Once the client has relaxed, rule out this possibility and remind them to raise their finger earlier, when they are slightly less relaxed.

Informal SCD

Informal SCD involves getting your client relaxed at, or near, the beginning of a session with the goal of maintaining that relaxation throughout the session. It is also intended to help them solidify the practice of keeping

> Strategy #7: Informal Self-Control Desensitization: To practice maintaining relaxation.

relaxed throughout the day such that it eventually becomes a habit. While formal SCD is intended to build the habit of catching anxiety spirals early, informal SCD is intended to build the habit of preventing the anxiety spirals by helping the individual to stay relaxed throughout the day. Nonetheless, informal SCD can also be a way to catch anxiety early, because there is a good chance that a spiral will begin during the course of any session–particularly when emotional and difficult topics are being discussed.

When conducting informal SCD, explain to your client when they arrive that you'd like to start with some relaxation. Be mindful that some clients come in eager to share something to "get it off their chest" or seek your advice. In these cases it may be difficult for them to relax and it may be best to give them time to unload. Once they have finished their story, you can ask if it would be all right if they waited to discuss the situation until after you've done relaxation. (If your client is verbose, such that they spend the first 15 minutes or more with talking, it may be a good idea to prepare them at the end of the previous session that you plan to do in-session SCD at the beginning of the next session. Explain that you'd like to do something new that will involve beginning the session with relaxation, but assure them that they will have plenty of time to talk.)

At this point, commence with meditation or relaxation. Once you conclude relaxation, have your client open their eyes and then check to see that they're relaxed. Then review the usefulness of maintaining relaxation throughout the day using frequent application of meditation and relaxation. Next explain that you are going to help them to practice that skill in the session today by periodically holding up a sticky note as a gentle reminder to stay relaxed.

Choose any simple form of relaxation or mindfulness that you use and ask your client to engage in that skill each time you raise your hand holding the sticky note. So, for instance, the following is a script starting after you've verified that they are relaxed:

We've discussed the importance of preventing anxiety from getting out of control by maintaining relaxation throughout the day. We are actually going to practice this skill of staying relaxed in the session today. So, as we talk about your week and things that you are worried about, I will periodically hold up this orange sticky note. When I do, this is a reminder to you to stay relaxed by letting go of any tension you don't need.

Hold up the sticky note every minute or two. You can also be strategic about when to hold it up. That is, if you see that your client is getting anxious by observing them tapping their foot or furrowing their brow, you can use this as an indicator that they aren't maintaining relaxation and that it is time to hold up the note.

About 10 minutes later switch the form of relaxation. You can also use acceptance if that has been helpful for the client in the past. Try to use at least three different forms of relaxation or acceptance. When using any form of breathing as relaxation, only hold up the sticky note when you are talking.

If they stop talking when you hold up the sticky note, remind them that the goal is to maintain relaxation throughout the day without stopping their flow of activity. Explain that if they feel like they need to stop every time they notice a sticky note, it will likely be counterproductive and annoying to the point where they may stop using them.

When doing either formal or informal SCD know that there are times when emotions are healthy. We don't want to help our clients repress healthy emotions. Sometimes it is better for our clients to feel their emotions (see Chapter 15). So, for instance, if a client comes in saying that their spouse was just diagnosed with cancer, processing this with them and normalizing emotion is important. I would really like to think that when we fully accept our emotions, the unhealthy part will melt away and the healthy part will continue. For example, Lindemann (1944) found that suppression of grief led to insufficient coping later in life. Pennebaker (1985) found that suppressing emotions following trauma, led to unhealthy physiological changes, including immune suppression, that led to medical conditions and that expression of emotion can improve immune function. See Chapter 15 for information about how repressing emotions interferes with healing GAD.

Whether doing formal or informal SCD we can use this as an assessment tool to determine which strategies are working best. When doing formal SCD, you can notice when the finger goes down and use this to guide you.

> Strategy #8: Self-Control Desensitization: Debrief to assess for most effective coping strategy.

For example, if you notice that when you say 'noticing the sound of the air conditioner' that they rapidly lower their finger, time after time, that it is an indication to guide them to focus on sounds. In particular, notice whether acceptance patter is useful (See Chapter 4).

With both formal and informal SCD, at the end of the session simply ask your client what they found to be most useful. If they hesitate, you may want to review the strategies that you used. Then guide them on how to apply those strategies throughout the day. So, for instance, you might say something like:

> *Great! We learned that focusing on the surfaces beneath you was particularly helpful. So I'm going to give you these orange sticky notes to put up in places that you see frequently and places that you associate with stress. When you notice them, gently shifting your focus to the surfaces beneath you. In addition, anytime you notice that you're beginning to feel anxious or even less relaxed, focusing on the surfaces beneath you.*

It's useful to give them the sticky notes you used in the informal SCD session. By the end of the session they have already begun a habit with that particular color and shape. Again, I believe the fact that it came from their therapist vs. their purchasing them or using some from work, adds particular value.

CHAPTER THREE

Don't Panic; Don't Worry – Not!

You're taking a walk or a run down a country road when you witness a driver turn down a muddy road and get stuck. You see him laying on the gas in a desperate attempt to get free only to see his wheels sink deeper and deeper into the mud. Later that day you see your nephew teasing his little brother saying his brain is the size of a pea. Your younger nephew takes the bait arguing, "It is not. Leave me alone. MOM!" You witness that the little boy's attempts to fight his brother backfire as he fuels his older brother to continue to taunt him. Worry and panic are similar to both of these situations. Attempts to fight anxiety are not only ineffective, they frequently exacerbate it.

In "the white bear research," Daniel Wegner (1987) found a paradoxical effect of thought suppression. After suppression of specific thoughts, they came back stronger. He asked one group of subjects to express their thoughts of a white bear followed by another period in which they were told to suppress thoughts of a white bear. Another group was told to suppress their thoughts of the white bear and then express thoughts of a white bear. First of all, when asked to suppress the thoughts, subjects were unable to suppress the thoughts, even after five minutes. Also, those who were asked to express their thoughts first expressed their thoughts progressively less, whereas those who were first asked to suppress their thoughts actually expressed these thoughts more over time. Subsequent studies indicated that this effect was even more pronounced when worry was substituted for the neutral white bear. In conclusion, when people simply try not to worry they will not be successful and they will be likely to worry even more later. Therefore, a common pitfall in the treatment of anxiety is teaching clients to push away anxiety and try to relax. In an effort to help clients ease their tension, worry less, and relax, many therapists unwittingly use commands such as "relax," "let it go," or "clear your mind." The use of commands in the course of leading meditation or relaxation can actually cause more anxiety or prevent relaxation. These approaches often lead to a similar scenario to the metaphor above in which spinning wheels in the mud results in staying stuck, or even worse digs one deeper in anxiety and frustration.

Depending on the client, I might add some humor and say *"Anyone ever tell you to relax and you want to flip 'em off?"* Or depending on the client, I might even say *"Anyone ever tell you to relax and you want to punch 'em?"* Everyone I've ever asked that question has smiled or laughed and said "yes." This is because not only is it true, it's funny that a suggestion to relax causes us distress. You want to flip them off, because they are telling you what to do; it's a command that creates tension. We don't like people to tell us what to do, especially when we're already feeling distress. Moreover, being told to "relax" can be extremely annoying as it seems to assume that we are over-reacting. So when we use those words in an effort to ease anxiety it's helpful to utilize process words instead of commands.

Of course, when clients use these words with their internal dialog, the effect is similar. In fact, it may be worse because many people are more critical of themselves than they are of others. It is best if clients experience the effect of "commands to relax" in the session. So I have them say the word "relax" and notice how it feels. Then I take a brief pause and ask them to say "relaxing" while noticing how it feels. I always use at least one more example while noticing how it feels. If it's a younger person, I usually use "chill out" and "chillin'." If it's an older person I might use "calm down" and "calming" or "let it go" and "letting go."

> Strategy #9: Use process words instead of command words to achieve relaxation.

Similar to avoiding commands, it is best to gently move toward relaxation rather than push away from anxiety. Instead of saying "clearing your mind" or "pushing away anxiety" use words that move towards relaxation. For example, "gently shifting your attention to the surfaces beneath you" or "observing your breathing." It takes more energy to push against something or fight something than it does to move toward something. Nonetheless, I will sometimes say "letting go of tension" as I believe we are much more capable of controlling tension in our bodies or other physical manifestations of anxiety than we are able to control thoughts. However, I rarely rely solely on "letting go of tension" such that I add something like "noticing how loose your body has become" or "feeling like a rag doll."

> Strategy #10: Moving toward relaxation rather than pushing away from anxiety to achieve relaxation.

To illustrate this concept further, here is an example script:

Old way: *Close your eyes. Clear your mind of worry. Let go of your tension. Notice the sounds in the room and outside the room. Notice the sound of your breathing and, at the same time, notice what you see, the back of your eyelids. Focus your attention on everything you see, hear, and feel.*

New way: *Gently closing your eyes. Moving your mind to the surfaces beneath you. Allowing any tension to drain into the couch, the pillows, the floor. Noticing the sounds in the room and those outside the room. Noticing the sound of your breathing and at the same time noticing what you see, the back of your eyelids. Focusing your attention on everything you see, hear, and feel. No matter where you are or what you are doing, noticing sounds, physical sensation, tastes, smells and sights.*

The aforementioned strategies are relaxation strategies that help the individual get out of their mind. When worrying uselessly about things that cannot be changed or controlled, these strategies are often the best way to free the mind. Certainly they are more effective than trying to not worry. However, when people are worrying about something that they have some control over, they may actually *want* to stay in their head. In some cases, letting go of the thoughts may be very threatening and cause an increase in anxiety because the worried client may feel like their concerns won't be resolved. After all, the most common reason people worry is probably to try to increase the likelihood that good things will happen and decrease the likelihood that bad things will happen. In other words, they are trying to solve a problem. So, instead of worrying or pushing anxiety away, help your clients to problem-solve. Don't worry; problem-solve.

When using problem solving as a strategy, it's useful to educate clients about the relationship between worry and problem solving.

> Strategy #11: Problem-solve instead of worrying.

People with GAD tend to be inflexible thinkers (Molina, Borkovec, Peasely, & Person, 1998) and have belief systems that aren't adaptive (Behar & Borkovec, 2002). Therefore they tend to have a difficult time problem solving. Interestingly, people with GAD are just as good at solving problems as their less anxious peers (Dugas, Letarte, Rhéaume, Freeston, & Ladouceur, 1995). However, worrying about what might happen and getting stuck on repetitive worries interferes with the ability to problem-solve. Similarly, anxiety interferes with concentration.

Almost everyone has experienced the relationship between problem solving and anxiety. Take for instance, trying to think of the name of something, whether it be a book title, an actor's name, or a city. You try so hard to remember the name and no matter how hard you try you usually cannot think of it. Then the instant you stop trying, voilá! There it is. Or a similar situation in which you are looking desperately for your keys because you are late. You look at all of the places that make sense, searching frantically. Then you remind yourself that your running around is futile and you allow your muscles to loosen and become more relaxed. As a result you remember that the last time you walked into the house you had to use the restroom. You find the keys sitting on the bathroom sink.

Creatives almost always say that they get their best ideas when they aren't looking for them. Paul McCartney had the entire melody to *Yesterday* come to him in a dream one night. In fact the tune came so easily that he was very concerned he had heard it elsewhere–that it wasn't his original song. So, for a few weeks, McCartney asked many people in the music business whether they had heard it. Moreover, for several weeks, the working title of the song was *Scrambled Eggs*. So when he and John Lennon *tried* to come up with lyrics, it obviously didn't come as easily or they wouldn't have had a working title of *Scrambled Eggs* for so long. This is just one of many examples of how the creativity that can be used to solve problems peaks during times of relaxation and is stunted by anxiety. *Yesterday* was voted the best pop song of all time by MTV and *Rolling Stone* magazine in 2000.

Some people with GAD may erroneously believe that their worry helps them to solve problems. This may be due to intermittent reinforcement, which is the most powerful type of operant conditioning. Despite

> Strategy #12: Convey the fact that worrying interferes with problem-solving.

the fact that worry interferes with problem solving, in the midst of worry, an occasional good idea will pop into one's mind: worry, worry, worry, worry, *good idea*, worry, worry, worry, etc. Worry is very much like golf. People who golf usually love golf and often find they can't get enough of it. I believe it's because of the intermittent reinforcement. With golf there is an okay shot, a bad shot, another bad shot, an okay shot, *a great shot*, an okay shot, an okay shot, etc. That occasional great shot keeps the golfer going back. Likewise, the occasional good idea in the midst of streams of worry, reinforces the habit of worry. Because worrying doesn't lead to good ideas, and there is actually evidence to the contrary, believing that worry is productive is superstitious as well.

In a nutshell, worry interferes with problem solving. It's ironic that worrying in an effort to achieve a goal is actually doing the opposite. In an effort to try to make things turn out better, worrying actually makes things worse. Much like the driver spinning his wheels in the mud, worry leads to becoming more and more stuck in one's problems. Not only does the worry reduce problem solving and concentration, it causes a great deal of useless discomfort (e.g., muscle tension, feeling keyed up/nervous). Presenting this rationale is the beginning of motivating clients to do a simple thing: problem-solve instead of worry. This information can also help clients to abandon anxious thoughts that are not useful in solving a problem. While this is certainly more easily said than done, there are a few strategies that you can try with your clients.

Problem-solving starts with the question: "What can I do about this?" Problem-solving is more effective when one allows their creative juices to flow by brainstorming many possible solutions to a problem without evaluating the utility of these solutions until later. For instance, let's say that your client's landlord won't fix the leaking ceiling despite their calling several times about the problem over the past couple of months. Your client is very frustrated and worries about whether the roof will ever get fixed. However, she hasn't tried anything besides calling the landlord every week or so and really hasn't generated any other strategies for getting it fixed. Yet she spends several hours a week worrying that the roof will cave in and feeling annoyed that nothing has been done.

We know from the creativity and problem-solving literature (Sawyer, 2007) that more creative problem-solving strategies come from having each person make their own list, than working together on a single list. So,

> Strategy #13: Brainstorm possible solutions and rate each one to arrive at a solution.

when a client has a worry that seems amenable to problem solving, take three to five minutes to independently generate a list. Then compile the two lists and brainstorm again. Sometimes, the other person's idea will spark your own creativity for another idea. So, once the list is compiled try to think of even more options together as you have them read off the list.

The following is a list of ideas for possible solutions to the leaking ceiling:

- refuse to pay rent until it's fixed
- write a letter to the landlord

- write a letter to the Better Business Bureau
- write a letter to both
- move out
- take photos of the leakage
- document all I am doing
- call daily until they fix it
- slap the landlord
- contact a lawyer
- have a friend call the landlord and pretend she's a lawyer
- contact tenants' rights for advice
- e-mail friends for ideas
- e-mail friends to see if they have any friends who are landlords and ask them what to do
- hire someone to fix it and deduct it from the rent
- fix it myself and deduct it from the rent
- get an estimate and write the landlord that I am going to have it fixed and deduct it from the rent if it's not fixed by a certain time
- threaten the landlord

Obviously, some of these ideas are ridiculous and unethical. However, sometimes outrageous ideas trigger thoughts of good ideas. At the very least they might help your client to laugh, vent, or both. You can get them to ask a friend or loved one to brainstorm a list as well. Remember to have them do their own list before looking at the other party's list. Given that people with GAD tend to have myopic thinking – that is, they usually see a limited scope of possibility – this is a great exercise to help them "exercise" creativity and open their eyes to several possibilities.

Once their list is made, it may be easy for your client to come to a decision about how to solve the problem. If they remain uncertain, you can help them to cross off the ideas that aren't ethical, are likely to cause more problems, or are otherwise poor choices. Next ask your client to rate the remaining items on a scale of 1 to 10, with "10" being an excellent idea and "1" being a bad idea. Choose the highest-scoring idea, or ideas, and if your client is still uncertain, discuss the feasibility and utility of the highest-rated ideas. Alternatively, they may choose to discuss the ideas with someone they respect or someone who will be affected by the decision. Below, see the list after the aforementioned process has occurred.

- refuse to pay rent until it's fixed 8
- write a letter to the landlord 4
- write a letter to the Better Business Bureau 5
- write a letter to both 5
- take photos of the leakage 7
- document all I am doing 7
- call daily until they fix it 3
- contact a lawyer 6
- contact a tenants' rights organization for advice 9
- get an estimate and write the landlord that I am going to have it fixed and deduct it from the rent if it's not fixed by a certain time 7

In this scenario, the person may decide to first call a tenants' rights organization in their area to see if they have advice. If they don't get any better ideas then they could refuse to pay the rent until it is fixed.

As discussed earlier, it is not only ineffective to try to not worry, it actually tends to potentiate worry. However, problem solving

> Strategy #14: Postpone Worry

can help. When problem solving isn't applicable or is otherwise ineffective, postponing worry is often very helpful. When a person feels unnecessarily pressed to solve a problem or make a decision, they don't have enough information, or are otherwise indecisive, postponing the worry can be most effective.

For example, Khadji was worried about whether to quit his job and move back home to Kenya. He missed his family terribly and was not as happy in Chicago as he thought he would be. However, he knew his career would not be as good in Kenya, and his wife didn't want to move back as most of her family lived outside of Kenya. He worried daily about this decision and lay awake many nights contemplating it.

After a discussion it was clear that Khadji wouldn't be able to move back for at least eight months due to commitments and red tape involved with returning to his home country. They had only moved to Chicago three months earlier. He missed his family much more since they had moved from Milwaukee where he had made some close friends. Yet he and his wife were not happy with their jobs there. After some discussion, he agreed that he really wouldn't start making arrangements to move back until two months beforehand. He agreed that in the next six to seven months he and his wife would have more information and that many things could happen in that time period. We decided he could postpone the decision for at least five months. This would give him and his wife at least a month to decide before it was even feasible to begin preparations to leave and more time if they wanted it. Therefore, we looked at the calendar and chose a date to which he postponed this worry. I instructed Khadji to write "Move?" on that date. In addition, we discussed that when he began to contemplate this decision he would gently remind himself that he had postponed making a decision to at least that date and would use additional coping strategies to let go of that concern. We also agreed that on that date he need not make a decision, but would start to contemplate it or postpone it again.

I changed the names and the cities, but this is based on an actual case and it was very effective. Any time that he started to think about it, he reminded himself that he didn't need to worry about it until the date he had recorded in his calendar. He followed this with mindfulness to effectively let go of the worry. Within a short period of time the worries were infrequent and fleeting. He actually "graduated" from therapy before the decision date as he had conquered that and his other worries.

This strategy to postpone worries is useful for many types of worries whether it's about something that has a date or not. If it's about the fear of a possible tragedy, postponing the worry to "if and when the tragedy happens," can be helpful. For example, many people worry about their spouse getting into a car accident. To postpone this worry when it surfaces, they can think "I'll worry about it if and when it happens." Short of making sure the tires are good or driving a safe car, there is nothing they can do. Helping to convince clients that worry will not help them to prepare for what might happen can be a useful addition.

Postponing worry is also very useful for continually postponing a decision. For instance, with Khadji, we could have had him contemplate his decision once a month (e.g. first Monday of each month) or even once a week. When doing this it is best to have clients write it in their calendar. I cannot emphasize enough that this strategy is very unlikely to work if the person doesn't fully intend to keep their worry and problem-solving date on the scheduled day. If they don't keep their problem-solving date, future attempts to postpone worry will probably not be effective.

When engaging in the worry/problem-solving period. We process better when we write and talk about our concerns too. I suggest writing each worry and saying it aloud and then writing and saying each problem-solving strategy. It is imperative that these worries not be addressed in a place where the client typically relaxes. So encourage them to find a place where they don't typically sit: the basement, a spare bedroom, or maybe a seat at the formal dining room where they don't sit. In smaller homes, choosing a place on the floor or moving a chair to a corner may be indicated. To enhance the ridiculousness of worry, you can also suggest going to a dry bath tub and sitting in there while fully clothed.

It can also be good to have a "relaxing chair." This is a place for your client to go to relax and disengage from their worries. They can practice meditation and other forms of relaxation or do something relaxing like reading or watching television. If they are unable to disengage from the worry while sitting in this chair, they are to quickly get up from the chair and go to the worry chair or to a more neutral space. Soon, this chair will become a stimulus for relaxation.

The postponement technique is also useful for daily worries. For example, worry about work and "to do lists." The commute is an excellent time in which to postpone worries. It is a great opportunity for busy people who don't want to make time for a worry period to attempt to solve problems, because they are held captive anyway. While driving a vehicle isn't a good place in which to write about worries, they can jot down some problem-solving ideas at stop lights.

Processing worries and paying them due diligence before bedtime or before an event is particularly helpful. Getting the worries "out of the way" beforehand, can help to prevent worries from interfering with sleep, improve concentration when needed, and increase enjoyment of leisure activities. I have developed a form that many clients find to be very useful in helping them to resolve worries before bed, before studying, before working, or before doing something relaxing (Abel, 2010). The client is to complete the first column by briefly writing about the thoughts that they are concerned will interfere with what they are getting ready to do. The second column provides a resolution before the event. The client is to write what he or she would like to do about the worries under the second column before engaging in the activity in which he or she is concerned worry will interfere. The form suggests three general choices: 1. Do something (i.e. take action before the activity) 2. Plan something (i.e. schedule an action to be done any time after the activity) 3. Do nothing before the activity. The decision to "do nothing" does not

> Strategy #15: Use the two column problem-solving form before bed, work, or event.

necessarily mean that the client has chosen never to do anything about the concern, rather they are choosing not to do anything about it before the event.

What I am likely to worry about:	What do I want to do about it before: (Choices: Do Something, Plan Something, Do Nothing)

To illustrate the use of this form, take the case of Hannah who is worried about finishing an important project that is due at the end of the week and is worried about the headaches she has been having. These two worries kept her awake the previous evening and she has been struggling with insomnia. She decides to utilize the problem-solving form before she relaxes for the evening. This is what it might look like:

What I am likely to worry about before bed.	What do I want to do about it before bed.
• Missing the deadline on Friday.	• Make a list of things to do to complete the project. • Divide them among the 3 days left. • Finish the draft. • E-mail Tom with questions.
• Headaches – Afraid it's something serious.	• Enter a reminder tomorrow to make an appointment with the doctor early next week.

As discussed previously, anxiety interferes with problem solving. The reverse is also true. Being relaxed can enhance creativity and help lead to problem solving. When clients

> Strategy #16: Use meditation to enhance problem solving.

are worried about a situation that is likely amenable to problem solving use a two-step process commencing after the client has presented the problem. First, use meditation or another form of relaxation and then ask your client to observe the problem without judgment in this relaxed state. If it's making a choice between two or more possibilities, then have them visualize choosing each option, noticing how they feel, and take time for relaxation in between visualizing each option. Similarly, encourage relaxation before engaging in a brainstorming session. Likewise, if your client feels most relaxed after a work-out, encourage him or her to engage in problem solving afterwards. One can integrate this idea into the problem solving form by relaxing between writing the worry and deciding on a plan. Finally, see strategy #22 on page 42 for another useful problem-solving idea.

CHAPTER FOUR

Mindfulness as Acceptance

Mindfulness is a mental state in which we are aware of thoughts, actions, or motivations. Mindfulness was born out of Buddhism and is an essential factor in the path to enlightenment. However, in recent years it has been used more and more in Western culture as a form of relaxation and acceptance. Jon Kabat-Zinn (1990) is often credited with bringing mindfulness to Western society. He, along with his colleagues at the Center for Mindfulness at the University of Massachusetts, has proven that mindfulness not only leads to a state of well-being and relaxation, but also to an improvement in a wide variety of performances, from those required of Olympic athletes, to those required in corporate jobs.

Mindfulness can be thought of as having two different kinds of benefits. One is a form of relaxation in which we focus on our senses to be "in the moment." (This will be covered in detail in the next chapter.) The present chapter covers the other: Mindfulness as acceptance. It involves observing discomfort, allowing it to be there, and resisting any urges to push it away. This often comes without effort for clients and is nothing short of magical. However, other clients have a very difficult time internalizing this practice and may never grasp it. I believe it's a concept that is more difficult to verbalize than any of the other strategies covered in this book. It's much more right-brained (non-verbal) and experiential, but unfortunately in this book and in therapy sessions we have to rely predominantly on verbal communication. In fact, after many years of practicing mindfulness and treating anxiety disorders, I still didn't fully understand it.

I'll never forget the time that I truly grasped the utility of mindfulness during a particular therapy session I had in the late 90's. I had been reading a book called *Going to Pieces Without Falling Apart: A Buddhist Perspective on Wholeness; Lessons from Meditation and Psychotherapy* (Epstein, 1998). While I was in the process of reading this book I was seeing a client whom I will call "Lindsey." She suffered from severe panic attacks several times per week and worried a great deal about having panic attacks. Within a few moments, Lindsey went from suffering from one of the worst cases of panic disorder that I had seen to being almost panic-free.

Lindsey arrived late, in the midst of a full-blown panic attack, and truly the worst panic-attack to date that I have witnessed. She sat on the edge of my couch, hyperventilating, crying, and barely able to speak. It took her a couple of minutes just to tell me that she almost didn't come, because she was so upset that she wasn't able to talk. My response was that it was okay, and I gave her permission to not talk. I suggested that we engage in relaxation. She refused, saying that there was no way she could possibly relax. I agreed that she was probably way too anxious to be able to benefit from relaxation. I was momentarily befuddled. I had this woman in my office crying, hyperventilating, and hysterical. She had refused my suggestion to engage in relaxation, and said she was too upset to talk. I thought, "What am I going to do? Sit here and watch her panic?"

Because I was in the midst of reading *Going to Pieces Without Falling Apart*, the concepts were fresh in my mind. Dr. Epstein did not discuss panic attacks or any specific "technique" to use to treat anxiety. So what I proceeded to do was inspired by his Buddhist-influenced work. Since then I have learned that many other therapists use similar forms of mindful acceptance in their practice. So this practice is neither mine nor Epstein's, but you can use it to effectively treat many clients with panic attacks. It can also be useful for other emotional states such as anger and depression.

I assured Lindsey that I wouldn't ask her to relax, but asked if she'd be willing to close her eyes. After she did, I proceeded by saying something like: "Observing where you feel the discomfort in your body. Noticing where the discomfort is located. Feeling how much space it takes up in your body. Letting go of trying to change it, but if it changes, allowing it to change. If it increases, let it increase, and if it decreases, let it decrease. Even though it's uncomfortable, allowing it to be there. Letting go of any struggle. Observing it almost as if you're an outsider looking in on the discomfort. Just continuing observing it and noticing how it feels. Letting go of any judgments about how you feel. Just observing how you feel and accepting it, even when it's uncomfortable." Her response was amazing!

Within two minutes Lindsey was grinning from ear to ear and soon she was laughing. She went from tears and hyperventilation

> Strategy #17: Mindful observation of emotion or physical sensations.

to a big smile and then excitement about this rapid transformation from terror to feeling fine, even happy. To my knowledge she never had an unexpected panic attack again and had very infrequent situational panic attacks. When she did have them they were "expected" in response to severe stressors. Even then they were significantly less severe and much shorter than she had suffered prior to this session. Lindsey was actually okay with these panic attacks because they were always in very stressful situations and still much milder and shorter than they had been in the past. Moreover, she no longer *feared* panic attacks. Most of this success was due to less than two minutes of acceptance therapy.

Lindsey's story appears to contradict completely the notion stressing early cue detection discussed previously. Certainly Lindsey's spiral was in the most advanced stage of anxiety. All coping strategies work best at the earliest events in the spiral – even acceptance. Mindful acceptance may be the one thera-peutic exception once the spiral is advanced. Of course it is easier to accept mild anxiety than severe anxiety. Nonetheless, acceptance can be very effec-tive even in the midst of a spiral that has a great deal of momentum. It can work faster than medication and without side effects and without negative reinforcement, because the individual is accepting the feelings fully rather than trying to escape them.

While the Buddhists may retain most of the credit for mindfulness, many Christians have learned the Serenity Prayer at an early age. Some people may be reluctant to engage in something associated with Buddhism if they are devout Christians. Therefore, if you are Christian or working with Christian clients, the Serenity Prayer may be more helpful in these cases: *God, grant me the serenity to accept the things I cannot change, The strength to change the things I can, and the wisdom to know the difference.* The phrase, *the strength to change the things I can* is consistent with the previous chapter's focus on problem solving.

Similarly, many people of any faith find peace in the practice of being able to "give it over to God." This is another way of relinquishing emotional strife and stress; put it in God's hands. While it's a different path to acceptance, it is trust and acceptance that God will take responsibility for outcomes such that the individual need not worry about them. For those who believe in the power of prayer, emotionally giving it over to God includes a form of acceptance that can immediately reduce distress, in addition to having faith that God will help.

Some people who have tried acceptance and found it ineffective, may have difficulty with acceptance because they misunderstand the concept. They might think or say, "I don't want to accept it; I want to change it or get rid of it." Be very clear about this: Acceptance does not mean that one is not going to try to change the situation. But when one is looking for solutions one will have more focus, patience, and creativity if one also accepts uncomfortable feelings and situations. In fact, Carl Rogers once said, "The curious paradox is that when I accept myself just as I am, then I can change." This is true of anxiety and other situations as well. When clients accept the feelings of anxiety and worry, the other strategies for reducing anxiety work better; it's easier to change things.

Another thing that can get in the way of acceptance and change is being overwhelmed by having too much one desires to change. Therefore, I have added a line to the serenity prayer such that it now reads:

> *God, grant me the serenity to accept*
> *the things I cannot change,*
> *The strength to change the things I can,*
> *the wisdom to know the difference,* and. . .
> The serenity to accept the things I'm in
> the process of changing or
> am not yet ready to change.

Regardless of one's religious or spiritual beliefs, the simplest way to experience acceptance of emotion and physical sensations of anxiety is to simply observe how it feels in the body. Help your client to observe that heavy feeling in their chest or that knot in their stomach and refrain from reacting to it in a negative way. If they *try* to push the anxiety away in the process it will prevent this strategy from being helpful. If they are able to observe those feelings without judgment and without fighting it, then they will have likely accepted it, and it is likely to diminish or even disappear completely. The following script is an example of how you might guide a client through mindful observation when they are feeling anxious or otherwise distressed:

> *Observing where you feel the discomfort in your body. Noticing how it feels. Observing how much space it takes up. Letting go of any judgments about how it feels. Resisting any habits of trying to pushing it away and even allowing it to stay. Noticing where it is located. Noticing the texture of how it feels. Observing what color it feels like it would be if you could see it. Letting go of any efforts to try to change it, but if it changes allowing it to change. If it increases, allowing it to increase, and if it decreases allowing it to decrease. Doing the opposite of trying to change it. Letting go of any effort to push it away yet*

avoiding trying to make it stay. Giving up any struggle. Just observing how you feel as if you're an outsider looking in.

"Awareness cures, trying fails," is a quote from a book called *A Soprano on Her Head* (Ristad, 1981) that sums up mindful observation when it works well. I recommend this book for musicians who are struggling with anxiety, whether it be performance anxiety or anxiety that is unrelated to music.

Observing anxiety often leads to auto-matic acceptance. However, sometimes ob-servation requires the added component of

> **Strategy #18: Acceptance of the situation.**

accepting the feelings to work well. There are two general things to teach clients to accept. The first, and most useful, is the situation itself. The second is the reaction to the situation as well as reactions to reactions, and so forth. For instance, your client spills coffee on their new pants. They can curse, blame themselves for being clumsy, get frustrated, and be really ticked off that the pants are stained or they can accept that there is nothing they can do to change the fact they spilled the coffee. In this situation, I like to ask, "What would you prefer? Would you rather spill coffee on your pants or spill coffee on your pants, be really upset by it, and let it ruin your morning or even your day?" In this particular example it is really best to accept the situation. In ad-dition, acceptance doesn't mean that they just leave the coffee on their pants. To the contrary, if they are accepting that this accident happened, it is more likely they will be quicker with problem-solving strategies and take action that might save the new pants. They will also save a lot of energy they'd waste by getting upset over something that they cannot change and that in the grand scheme of things is not all that important.

However, it's certainly natural for anyone to feel annoyed or frustrated by having spilled coffee on their new pants. This is particularly so if they're going somewhere they want to look nice and aren't at home where they can change or if taking time to change would cause them to be late. Similarly, it's very common and normal to feel anxious in many situations like meeting someone new for the first time, going on a job interview, or being lost. There are individuals who are able to maintain a sense of equanimity by completely accepting these types of situations, having internalized the uselessness of get-ting upset. For those who are not able to accept the situation, the next best thing is accepting the emotions that follow in these understandably frustrat-ing, anxiety-producing, or otherwise distressing situations.

Try to help your clients accept the situation, but when they are unable to accept the situation, because they feel powerless to control their emotion, help them learn to accept their emotion. So I might ask the question: "Would you rather be anxious or would you rather be anxious and frustrated that you're anxious?" If you can't accept the situation and feel frustrated or anxious as a result, accept it rather than getting more anxious and frustrated and possibly adding layers of additional emotions onto that. For example, you might start to get anxious that you're frustrated and depressed that you're anxious and frustrated. Even when there are layers of uncomfortable emotion any level of acceptance is helpful. Remember Lindsey. Layers of reactions including anxiety, frustration, and sadness melted away when she accepted them.

Acceptance is helpful with many emotions. I work primarily with people who are
suffering from anxiety disorders, which is why

> Strategy #19: Acceptance of emotion.

I first found amazing success with this technique for someone having a panic attack. But acceptance can work just as well with frustration, job tension, family stress, sadness, and many other problems.

Earlier in this chapter, observation of feelings and physical sensation were used as a way to mindfully accept emotion. Another very useful tool in diminishing, and often stopping, worry is mindful observation of thoughts. Some people find that by just observing their thoughts, almost as if they are an outsider looking in on the thoughts, their minds clear on their own accord.

Thought observation is so simple that many clients have difficulty with it. It simply involves observing the thoughts that are going on in one's head. Despite my saying, "avoiding trying to think and trying to *not* think," clients often feel obliged to think and try to continue to worry. They may do the opposite and try to clear their thoughts. Therefore, precede thought observation with purposeful worry. Otherwise clients may start to question the purpose of the exercise. In other words, if you say, "I'd like for you to close your eyes and just observe your thoughts" the client will be more likely to begin to question the rationale for doing the exercise. They might think, "why is she having me do this?" In addition, it is best to begin with, "I'd like to do a little experiment and then I will lead you into some relaxation." Finally, I believe that clients are more likely to respond if the concept of acceptance is explained after the exercise. Otherwise they are likely to try too hard and interfere with just observing their thoughts. The following is an example of what I might say after I've explained that we're doing a little experiment after which we will do relaxation.

> *I'd like for you to close your eyes and purposefully begin to think about*
> *something that you have been worried about that you have wanted to*

stop thinking about. [You might ask him or her to worry specifically about something discussed earlier in the session.] (pause) *Observing the thoughts that are going on in your mind.* (pause) *From here on out avoiding trying to think and avoiding trying to not think. Instead, being a passive observer by just noticing the thoughts that are going on in your mind without judgment. You may be inclined to try to think or you may be inclined to try to put the thoughts out of your mind. Doing neither. Letting go of all effort except observing and accepting any thoughts that go through your mind.* (pause) *Observing these thoughts almost as if you're an outsider looking in, almost as if you're watching cars drive down the street or birds flying.* (20-30 sec pause) *Continuing to just observe the thoughts.* (pause for an additional 20-30 sec)

Some anxious clients respond very well to only observing their thoughts and will experience a reduction or cessation of worries.

> **Strategy #20: Observation of thoughts.**

These clients often automatically begin to focus on their senses and some will experience pleasant images or see colors. Still others will have more positive or more adaptive thoughts than they had been experiencing. Unfortunately, some clients find thought observation useless, and it may even increase the thoughts. When the response is unfavorable, adding labels can be very helpful.

After I have a client simply observe the thoughts and before introducing relaxation, I introduce labeling the thoughts. Often, those who did not respond to merely observing, find that their worries decrease when we objectify those thoughts by labeling each one (Abel, 2010). First I simply ask that they label each thought as either a "new" thought or a "repeat" thought. Of course, most "repeat" thoughts are worries. And almost every worry is a repeat thought except the very first time it is a thought. I recommend following thought labeling immediately after thought observation while the client's eyes are still closed. Here is an example of a script for thought labeling:

Soon I'm going to ask you to label each thought that comes into your mind as being either "new" or "repeat": "repeat" if you've had the thought before, "new" if it's a new idea or fresh perspective. If you're not certain, don't get stuck on deciding; rather label it as "new." Continuing to just observe your thoughts. Avoiding trying to think and avoiding trying to not think, but after each thought that comes into your mind label the thought aloud as either "new" or "repeat" starting now.

Often after labeling a thought as "repeat" several times, worriers begin to experience their thoughts in a new way, one in

> **Strategy #21: Label each thought as "new" or "repeat."**

which they not only know in their mind that repetitive worries are useless,
but they finally feel the futility of their worry as never before. The result is
often that the worries are decreased and often stop involuntarily such that
their mind goes blank. It is also common for once worried individuals to find
themselves thinking about pleasant images. Sometimes even people who have
never heard of mindfulness, find their minds naturally moving away from
thoughts and onto their senses. For example, following a query about what the
"new" thoughts were, clients often say something like, "I'm noticing the sound
of the air-conditioner" or, "I thought, wow, this is cool, my mind went blank."

Other labels besides "new" and "repeat" can be helpful. It is best to begin
with "new" and "repeat," because they are simple and less likely to be judged
by a client who is self-critical. Nonetheless, some people respond much better
to the labels "useful" and "useless." When it works, the idea of repeating "useless" thoughts resonates and helps the worried client to disengage better than
recognizing a "repeat" thought. However, self-critical people will sometimes
get frustrated with themselves when using labels like "useless," because they
judge themselves for thinking so many "useless" thoughts. Furthermore with
the useful/useless labels, some thoughts fall into a third category of "neutral"
with useless thoughts being worries, useful thoughts being problem-solving or
positive thoughts that help, and neutral thoughts being neither (e.g., I'm hungry). Therefore I like the simplicity of the dichotomy of "new" and "repeat."

There are many other pairs of labels you can use such as "wanted" and
"unwanted," "pleasant" and "unpleasant," "worry" and "other," or "silly" and
"healthy." Labeling thoughts as being about the "present," "past," or "future,"
can be very helpful. There are numerous other possibilities. I encourage you
and your client to develop labels that suit them best.

In the last chapter, the utility of problem
solving as an alternative to worry was presented.
An additional way to problem-solve is to ask
your client to observe a specific issue that

> **Strategy #22: Use labels of "useful" and "useless" for problem solving.**

they are worried about and soon ask them to label each thought that they
are having about the issue as being "useful" or "useless." While there are no
guarantees, often people will begin to label their thoughts as "useful" and,
upon reflection, find they have solved the problem or developed a better
perspective. For instance, I recently used this strategy with a client who was
organizing an important out-of-town meeting, having her say the labels aloud.

After saying "useless" four or five times, she said "useful." Upon reflection of the exercise she was smiling. She said that her biggest worry was that she wouldn't be prepared. After realizing the futility of these thoughts, she automatically relaxed and then she solved the problem without even trying which was: "I will prepare for the meeting." She also had the positive thought that she had plenty of time in which to prepare and, after opening her eyes, she realized that her meetings always turned out better than she had feared.

These labels, particularly the "useful" and "useless" labels or the "silly" and "healthy" labels can be applied to physical sensations of anxiety and other useless emotions. This is particularly useful for individuals who state

> Strategy #23: Label physiological symptoms of anxiety as "useful" or "useless."

that they don't notice active worries, rather they feel the weight of their stress in their bodies. However, for most individuals it is recommended that you start with labeling thoughts and once the habit of labeling is pretty solid begin to label emotions.

The concept of mindful acceptance is one that I have found can come very easily, but often requires significant effort. Some people are not able to benefit from it. I think there are two reasons why acceptance is challenging. The first is that those who are unable to benefit are still trying to make the discomfort go away and unable to relinquish that struggle. It's the struggle that will often fuel the discomfort. Although they are trying to accept it, they are more focused on making it go away. It won't work if they try to accept it only because they are trying to make it go away or if they get frustrated that it's not going away. If this is what they are doing, they are not accepting it. In fact, they're doing the opposite of accepting it. There has to be a willingness to actually feel it.

Steven Hayes (2005) has a section in his book *Get Out of Your Mind and Into Your Life* that is headlined: "If you don't want it you will." He goes through the mind of someone with anxiety processing this information. The person thinks: "If this concept is true, then the reverse must be true. That is that if I am willing to have anxiety, I won't have anxiety." It's not that easy, because if they are only willing to have anxiety in order to *not* have anxiety then they are not truly willing to have anxiety. The trick with mindful acceptance is truly being willing to accept anxiety. The paradox is that once one is able to accept anxiety, it dissipates.

Another reason people have a difficult time grasping the experience of acceptance is that the process is wordless and it is not visual; it's more kinesthetic and emotional. Someone can show you and tell you how to drive a car.

Similarly, you can teach and demonstrate to a client how to breathe in a relaxing way. Acceptance is different. Words, pictures, and diagrams are often inadequate to explain the experience of acceptance. The other concepts in this book are much more easily conveyed, because I am able to specifically explain the approach in a concrete and clear manner with words. In a way, teaching acceptance is like trying to explain color to someone who can only see black and white.

It's best if you have an opportunity to catch your clients in the midst of being worried and anxious. This is the true test of whether or not he or she will easily benefit from acceptance of anxiety. Alternatively you can attempt to trigger anxiety in the session with interoceptive exposure (See Chapter 9). Once you have had a chance to experiment in the session you should know rather quickly whether your client is able to accept their thoughts and emotions or not. Alternatively, you can make a recording of acceptance patter for them to listen to when they are anxious.

METAPHORS AND EXAMPLES

For those who struggle with the concept of acceptance, different examples and metaphors are often the key to grasping the process. Different people connect with different metaphors. Therefore several metaphors are presented to increase the likelihood that one of them will resonate. One of the following metaphors is likely to help your clients to internalize the concept of acceptance and use it effectively.

Metaphor One: The Chinese Finger Trap

My mentor during my postdoctoral fellowship at Penn State, Tom (T.D. Borkovec), used two examples to explain acceptance and illustrate its utility. One example is the Chinese finger trap. (See photo below). You can see the uselessness of the struggle. The harder one tries to pull his or her fingers apart the more stuck one becomes. Relief is experienced only from giving up the struggle; relief is realized from surrendering. Many of us feel that surrendering is quitting or leaving us vulnerable. Not only is this untrue, but often the alternative is to continue a useless struggle that only makes matters worse. Furthermore, with anxiety and with the Chinese finger trap, once we accept it we are more relaxed and thereby in a better position to be able to let go (escape the finger trap) or deal with the situation. Eifert and Heffner (2003) found that teaching this simple strategy led to significantly greater reduction in avoidance, anxiety symptoms, and anxious thoughts than teaching breathing retraining. It is best that you actually demonstrate this concept by purchasing a Chinese finger trap and letting your clients experience it for themselves.

Metaphor Two: Bees

The second metaphor Tom Borkovec used was bees. Say you are sitting outdoors and five or six bees are swarming around you. Depending on your experiences in the past, you are likely to have at least a small degree of discomfort about the bees. If you surrender, the bees will not likely sting you and they might even settle down a bit if you are settled. If you start to swat at the bees, or try to kill them, you are much more likely to irritate them. They will fly faster and buzz louder. Not only will this exacerbate your distress, but also you will certainly increase the risk that they will sting you.

Metaphor Three: The Devil's Snare

Given that acceptance is a difficult concept to learn, I'd like to add a fantastic example from a film that is particularly useful for Harry Potter fans of all ages, particularly older children and adolescents. In the first Harry Potter book and film, *Harry Potter and the Sorcerer's Stone*, Harry, Hermione, and Ron find themselves in a position where they need to make a steep jump to safety and find themselves trapped in a large number of what appear to be tree roots called *Devil's Snare*. Hermoine urges the others to relax because she knows that the more one struggles to get out of the roots, the tighter the Devil's Snare will squeeze. She then relaxes and is released beneath the roots. Harry follows the advice, relaxes, and is soon released. Ron, however, continues to struggle, being grasped tighter and tighter by the Devil's Snare roots until Hermione remembers that the Devil's Snare weakens with bright light.

Stress and anxiety are often similar to the Devil's Snare such that the more one struggles to escape, the more one is bound by it. Some people are able to accept and relax despite intense circumstances, much like Hermione and Harry; others, unfortunately, are more like Ron, fighting it only to feel worse.

Metaphor Four: Charley Horse

Most people have experienced a charley horse (a painful cramp in the calf). I remember the first time I had one. I was a little girl, probably about six or seven years old. I was playing on the sidewalk near our back door. Suddenly I felt this gripping, intense pain in my calf. I was terrified! I screamed. I cried. I was afraid that there was something horribly wrong with my leg. My mom came running out to see what was wrong and when I told her, she said something like, "Oh, Jennifer, that's just a charley horse. It's normal. Sometimes people will get a cramp in their leg that hurts really badly, but it's nothing to be worried about." From then on, I accepted such calf cramps. They hurt every bit as much, but they never again scared me, and I have never cried or screamed about them since that day. Once you have accepted the pain, it's easier to make the cramps go away by stretching those muscles by pointing your toes toward your head.

Most people have experienced these cramps and remember how painful they can be. However, it is likely that these cramps have not triggered any significant anxiety in your clients despite how uncomfortable they are. They are likely more physically painful than any anxiety or frustration symptom they are experiencing. Therefore, drawing the analogy between the uncomfortable physical sensations often brought on by worry (e.g. muscle tension, heaviness in the chest, or a knot in the stomach) or the more intense symptoms that occur during the course of a panic attack (e.g., chest pain, tachycardia, dyspnea) with a charley horse can be helpful. Encourage them to accept these symptoms much in the way they would accept a charley horse. Explain that if they are able to accept the anxiety symptoms in this way they are very likely to decrease or even go away. It is this response of observing the discomfort and accepting it that can help to decrease or eliminate the intensity. If your client wears stilettos, or similarly uncomfortable pretty shoes, this can also be a great analogy as can the discomfort of a sunburn, eating too much, or being really cold. Chances are at least one of these physically uncomfortable situations will resonate with a particular client.

Metaphor Five: The Antagonistic Sibling

Whether you have been an antagonistic sibling, have survived an antagonistic sibling, or have witnessed this relationship in others, it's very clear that fighting against the antagonism fuels it. A child who doesn't understand that ignoring or even encouraging the antagonism from their typically older brother or sister, will take away their power. This is analogous with an anxiety sufferer who continues to try to fight their anxiety. In both cases, their efforts to resist the discomfort actually make it worse.

When I was a child, my brother would draw pictures of ugly witches and write my name beneath it. I got so frustrated when my mom would say "ignore him." As an adult not only do I see that she was right, I know that a certain way to get him to stop would have been to say something like, "Wow, that looks just like me! Can I keep that?" or better yet pose and ask him to draw my profile next. Anxiety is very much the same. If we allow it to be there or even try to increase it, it often melts away.

Metaphors: Concluding Thoughts

Hopefully one of the metaphors above will resonate with each of your clients. If not, there are probably other metaphors regarding acceptance. In fact, a recent client who was unable to connect with the aforementioned metaphors, connected with the metaphor of an undertow suggested by her psychiatrist. An undertow is an underwater current flowing violently away from the ocean shore as a result of wave force. When one fights this current they get stuck in it and can drown. The key is to "go with the flow" of the water and once released swim vertically with the shore. Therefore, continue to look for other metaphors that may resonate with your clients.

ACCEPTING HEALTHY EMOTIONS

Cognitive-behavioral therapy receives significant criticism from more traditional psychotherapists that it ignores emotion and even masks it. While I believe it is good to let go of unhealthy emotion, there are times when our emotions run high, and it's healthy to experience them. Although you might argue that it's natural and healthy to be frustrated after spilling coffee on your pants, I'm talking about more difficult situations, like grief. In the following situation it would be normal and healthy to feel emotion and you would not expect acceptance to free you from pain:

> *Bill's dog runs around in the front yard where he has installed an electric fence. Imagine that someone comes speeding through his neighborhood, loses control of the car, and kills Bill's dog. It's unlikely that he could accept this situation and feel no emotion. In fact, if he did respond this way it would be of particular concern that he is numb and has serious deeper emotional issues. It is likely that anyone in Bill's*

situation will feel very sad about his or her dog and that anger toward the speeder would ensue. In this situation, it is best for Bill to accept his emotions and feel them. Unlike the spilled coffee situation, in these tragic situations acceptance will not release anger and sadness, because these stronger emotions are healthy.

If healthy anger and sadness are not accepted, other emotions that are unhealthy are very likely to be experienced. By helping clients to accept healthy emotions you can help them prevent unhealthy emotions from taking over. Their initial reactions are often healthy; it's the reactions to the emotions that are typically unhealthy. Marsha Linehan (1993) re-

> Strategy #25: Accepting primary emotions.

fers to these emotions as primary and secondary emotions. Primary emotions are healthy emotions, while secondary emotions are the reactions to these emotions. I believe that the secondary emotions occur as a result of unhealthy *cognitions* usually stemming from rejecting the primary emotions. For instance, Bill might feel embarrassed when he starts to cry because he believes that men shouldn't cry. He may then get frustrated with himself and prevent the processing of the healthy primary emotions of grief and anger.

Approach primary emotions in a Socratic fashion. For instance, ask Bill: "What emotions do you believe everyone would feel if their dog were killed by a speeder?" Of course most people would get angry and sad if a speeder killed their dog. Normalizing their emotions can better help clients to accept these primary emotions such that unhealthy cognitions and unhealthy secondary emotions don't emerge.

Regardless of whether or not emotions are healthy in a particular situation, if your client cannot accept the situation, help him or her to accept their feelings. Often if we completely accept our emotions about a trying situation, the unhealthy emotions will disappear and the remaining healthy emotions will persist in order to help us protect ourselves and allow healthy grief reactions. When we lose someone close, even the healthiest people feel sadness. Fear and anger can often help us to protect ourselves. Once we accept circumstances and emotions, it is usually easier to take action and, if warranted, work to change the situation.

THE ROLE OF COGNITION IN ACCEPTANCE

Acceptance doesn't require cognitive therapy or any direct changes in thought. Actually, acceptance does not require words at all. However, negative thought patterns like: "I can't accept it. It's awful. I need to get rid of this anxiety" will certainly prevent clients from being able to benefit from acceptance. Therefore, in instances in which your client is having difficulty with acceptance, adding a cognitive therapy piece to help them to change their thoughts may help to open the door to making acceptance possible.

When you believe negative cognition is playing a role in preventing acceptance, help clients to reflect upon a recent situation in which something was frustrating or anxiety-producing without their having any control over the outcome. Or wait until they share such a situation and utilize cognitive therapy. For instance, if Brandon went through a yellow light that was on camera, and he worried that he was going to get a ticket, he might have difficulty accepting the situation due to persistent thoughts like: "What if I get a ticket? It will cost me points on my license. It will cost me money. My insurance premium will go up." These thoughts may make it impossible to accept the anxious feelings about being caught. In this instance, cognitive therapy may aid Brandon in the acceptance process. Perhaps the Socratic question of: "What do you stand to gain from worrying about this?" may be helpful. If not, perhaps reminding him that worry will not make it any less likely that he'll get a ticket will be helpful. You might even ask him something like this: "If you do get the ticket, would you rather get a ticket or would you rather worry about getting the ticket *and* get a ticket? And if you don't get the ticket, will you be glad that you worried about it? Do you stand to gain anything by worrying about the ticket?" After "softening" with cognitive therapy, acceptance may be more useful.

Not only do negative thoughts make it more difficult to be accepting, but learning to be more accepting is likely to improve the nature of problematic thoughts. For instance, when Lindsey experienced relief, she smiled and then said what she was thinking. It was something like, "I felt the permission to feel what I was feeling and so I stopped beating myself up. Now I know that it is okay to have some feelings of distress, and it doesn't need to be awful."

CHAPTER FIVE

Relaxation

We experience fear and anger to protect ourselves. When faced with stressful circumstances, whether it's fear, anxiety, anger, or frustration, our bodies react with a sympathetic nervous system response, otherwise known as the "fight or flight response." This response "gears up" our bodies to help us fight or run as a means of protecting ourselves against danger.

This physiological response occurs regardless of whether we are being faced with a physical threat or an emotional threat. Whether our clients experience a sympathetic nervous system response because they are being chased by an attacker or because they are in an unhealthy relationship or are overwhelmed with a long "to-do list" their bodies will respond in a similar way to each stressor. If our bodies were designed perfectly, emotional stressors would produce a different response from physically threatening stressors. It would help us to appropriately change or avoid emotionally unhealthy situations without the excessive energy and physical discomfort associated with a significant sympathetic nervous system response that is ironically meant to protect us from danger. When clients have panic attacks they feel as though they are in danger when they are not. It's a false alarm.

Explain to your client that their bodies are actually responding in a healthy way to fear or frustration, but that because their stressors are largely psychological, those responses are useless. In fact, the labels of "useful" and "useless" with regard to physical symptoms of anxiety may work better once your client understands this. Explaining that the fear response that their ancestors had when being chased by a natural predator, the feelings of anxiety they experienced was very adaptive. Whether it be a bear chasing us or psychological threat the sympathetic nervous system response sets off a number of physiological reactions in our bodies to help us physically protect ourselves. Our breathing increases to get more oxygen into the bloodstream, our heart pumps faster to get more blood to our arms and legs, and tension in those muscles increases so we can fight better and run faster. Our pupils dilate to

53

allow in more light so we can see more clearly, particularly in darker places. Even the sweat on our hands helps our fingerprints to grip better to climb or use a weapon. In summary, fear can actually protect us when the threat is a physical one.

Unfortunately, most of the time that our clients experience these physiological changes in their bodies, it is in response to an emotional threat. In these situations in which there is not physical danger, they feel wound up with no place to go. Their bodies are geared up and prepared to fight and run, but there is nobody there to physically fight and, in most situations, nowhere to run. The feelings are not only useless, they are also physically and emotionally detrimental, causing discomfort and draining energy.

On the one hand, sympathetic nervous system responses can be useful when our clients are in a place that is psychologically unhealthy. I have seen numerous people whose anxiety or anger was manifesting itself in their body as an indication that they needed to leave a relationship, leave a job, or find more balance in their lives. This is a reason that I sometimes discourage people with mild to moderate levels of depression, anger, and anxiety from taking medication. It may help them to tolerate being in a situation that is unhealthy for them and prevent them from making a healthy change. The uncomfortable feelings they have are often a warning response that can help to motivate them to change their situation with some help from you. I'm sure you have heard someone say "get out of that relationship" or "run from that job." So, despite the fact that our nervous systems are not optimally designed for dealing with psychological threat, the discomfort can help motivate our clients to leave a job, end a relationship, or make other positive changes in their lives.

On the other hand, most of the time the tension and stress our clients carry in their bodies due to the sympathetic nervous system response is useless. More often than not our situations are healthy enough that leaving them is not the answer. Rather, the emotional responses to the workload and schedule, for example, lead to more muscle tension, stress, and worry than is needed to handle them. Most of the people we see want to stay in their jobs and in their relationships, but their stress levels are out of control. Their sympathetic nervous systems are gearing them up to fight and run, when all they need to do is walk. I don't mean walk literally, but figuratively. That is, take a walking pace in accomplishing things. Instead our clients often are running blindly when what the situation really demands is to sit and talk, sit and work on the computer, engage in meetings, drive, engage in a disagreement, and so forth.

Once you have helped your client to identify their stressors (i.e., situations that cause stress), help them to decide whether it is best to change the stressor (e.g., leave their job) or change their reaction to the stressor (apply the strategies in this book). Whether it is a relationship, work, school, or another situation that brings people to therapy, the following approach is often useful: "How about we start by doing what we can to help you manage your stress, problem solve, and change your life for the better, and if the change isn't great enough we can work on changing your situation?" When clients are contemplating ending their marriage, for instance, I might encourage them to try couples therapy and, if that isn't effective, they often feel better about leaving the marriage.

Excessive reactions to ordinary daily stressors drains more energy than our clients need to use in order to get through the day. It may be due to breathing too fast or by carrying that uncomfortable feeling in their chests. Having irritable bowel symptoms can also drain energy. One of the most common reactions to stress is excess muscle tension from their bodies preparing them to fight and run. Our muscles run throughout the entire body. Therefore, excess muscle tension can cause considerable discomfort and cause significant fatigue. Most people use more tension than they need to perform any given task, whether it's a very intense physical task or something as easy on the body as reading a book or watching TV. For example, right now, at this moment, ask yourself this question: "Do I need all of this tension to read this book?" See if you can let go of the excess tension in your body. When presenting this concept to clients I recommend asking them if they need all of the tension they are using to sit in therapy and ask them to see how much tension they can release without falling over.

We have established that our nervous systems are not designed to deal with the stressors of modern society. Because our nervous systems are designed to protect us from physical threat, when we experience mental stress we often have excess energy that can cause discomfort, and fatigue, and wreak havoc on our health causing or contributing to a host of medical problems. It follows that relaxation designed to attenuate the physiological effects of anxiety will be helpful.

One limitation of the way that relaxation is typically delivered by therapists and practiced by clients is that it's short-lived. Even those who are able to get deeply relaxed after several minutes of engaging in a relaxation exercise find that the relaxation often disappears completely within the course of a few minutes and seldom lasts more than a couple of hours. So continue to keep in mind the importance of teaching our clients to utilize relaxation throughout the day.

Another problem with relaxation is that many of the most stressed people actually get more stressed at the thought of closing their eyes and relaxing for several minutes. This is often due to a drive to succeed and a fear of wasting time, but it may also be because relaxing leads to increased vulnerability. Some clients' worried minds are far too busy to make it possible to focus long enough to relax, and the effort put forth without success leads to frustration.

It's important to recognize that many individuals either have too much competing anxiety to be able to relax quietly, they have ADHD, or otherwise have difficulty concentrating. Therefore, when teaching relaxation understand that some people actually need some stimulation in order to relax. For instance, some people feel that they are most relaxed when running. It is our job as therapists to help them to actually create the type of stimulation that can be relaxing, or help them to capitalize on activities in which they are already engaging (e.g., running, gardening, playing music) as part of their relaxation practice. In addition, even those who relax best with peace and quiet, will want to learn to be able to relax in the face of challenging and stressful situations.

After reading Chapter 1, you have become aware of the importance of catching anxiety early. Likewise, you learned the utility of practicing relaxation throughout the day in order to maintain a level of peace and prevent anxiety spirals from the beginning. Once again, the key is to teach your clients to relax multiple times throughout the day, without stopping their usual flow of activity. Nearly all therapists teach at least some relaxation or meditation as part of their practice, so hopefully you have already begun teaching your clients the art of preventing anxiety from getting out of control. In this chapter, I will share some of the relaxation tools that I utilize to help people relax.

MUSCLE RELAXATION

Progressive Relaxation (PR) is likely the most effective relaxation technique for people to learn (Bernstein & Borkovec, 1973). How-

> Strategy #26: Progressive Relaxation

ever, even after learning in graduate school how to teach this procedure, I learned from Tom Borkovec that I had not been using it to its fullest potential. A complete training on PR is beyond the scope of this book, so I recommend that you read the follow-up PR manual (Bernstein, Borkovec, & Hazlette, 2000). In short, PR involves systematically tensing and releasing 16 muscle groups such that the individual learns to feel the difference between tension and relaxation and is able to lower his or her adaptation level (i.e., the amount of tension one uses to get through the day). PR offers many salubrious effects including a positive effect on: sleep, tension headaches, blood pressure, pain, anxiety, sexual satisfaction, and irritability. Remember when conducting PR to use process words in your patter (e.g. letting go, visualizing your muscles loosening, smoothing out, unwinding).

Whether you already utilize PR in your practice, or you plan on reading the manual, or both, the following more brief muscle relaxation strategies will work much better if PR is also taught. Dr. Borkovec believes that it is imperative to practice the full 16-muscle group PR practice twice daily for at least two weeks before moving on to the shorter seven-muscle group practice. While this is optimal, I will skip teaching traditional PR and instead move forward with the following strategies only if the person is unwilling to set aside about 20 minutes required to practice PR at least daily. Sometimes I make exceptions and start with the seven-muscle group that is traditionally taught only after the 16-muscle group is mastered. These exceptions include being willing to put aside 10 minutes/day or when people have ADHD and can maintain much better focus on the shorter task. All of the following strategies can be helpful without teaching PR when PR is not indicated.

Differential relaxation (Bernstein & Borkovec, 1973) is typically taught in the next session after teaching full progressive relax-

> **Strategy #27: Differential relaxation**

ation. It can be taught without PR, but will likely be less effective. It involves practicing engaging in a number of activities while using the least amount of tension possible. This process begins by asking the individual to keep sitting just as they are while letting go of any unnecessary tension in their body. Often this works best by simply asking: "Do you need all of the tension you have in your body now?" They reflexively will let go of much of the tension. Then say, "letting go of any tension in your legs (pause) arms (pause) face and neck (pause) and torso." Then have your client reposition to feel more comfortable. That is, have them sit in a way that there are surfaces supporting their limbs, back, head, and neck.

The next step of differential relaxation is to ask clients to stand up using the least amount of tension without falling down and still holding up their head. Then asking them where they need no tension. The answer is arms, face, and shoulders. Next ask: "Where do you need tension?" The answer is feet, legs, spine, and neck. Then ask if they can let go of half of their tension in their legs. Then ask the same with feet, spine, and neck – all using the least amount of tension without falling down.

Next, walk at a normal pace with the least amount of tension and then at a quick pace. You might ask your client to write something (their biggest worry or an adage like: "a stitch in time saves nine"). Then have them rewrite with the same speed, maintaining penmanship, but using the least amount of tension. If they have a laptop, you could ask them to use it in a similar manner. Ergonomics is a corollary of differential relaxation which is particularly important for people with desk jobs who sit at their computer most of the time. If people are fighting gravity or otherwise sitting in an unhealthy position, the utility of differential relaxation will be limited. Many companies will order an ergonomic assessment for their employees, particularly with a doctor's order.

For clients who complain of fatigue, present the concept of energy conservation. Encourage them to use reminders to question whether they need all of the energy they are using or to ask themselves "What's the least amount of energy I can use at this moment?" The idea is to use less energy without sacrificing performance. The result is that performance is enhanced due to the prevention of fatigue later in the day.

A very quick way to release muscles is "tin man-to-scarecrow," which I developed for people who do not want to learn PR due to

> **Strategy #28: Tin Man to Scarecrow**

the time commitment but have considerable muscle tension (Abel, 2010). However, it can be helpful for people who practice PR too. It involves tensing all of muscles in the body like a tin man. (Tin, because one can get hurt trying to tense too much.) Instruct clients to tense about 50-75% of maximum rather than tensing as hard as they can like an iron man. (Before beginning, ask your client if they have any injuries or pain. Like PR, tin man to scarecrow should never cause pain. Tell your clients that if tensing causes pain that they should back off to the point of only mild discomfort). The first step is to tense all of the muscles in the body including the face, neck, feet, and torso for about 10 seconds. The next step is "letting go" of all of the muscles, feeling like a scarecrow, no joints, loose, and letting the surfaces beneath support the entire body. Repeat, and if muscles are still tense, then you can focus just on the areas that are still tense.

Relaxation imagery I developed called "the sponge" is effective for many people. For this particular technique, see to it that your

> **Strategy #29: Sponge Imagery Relaxation**

client's body is completely supported by the surfaces beneath them. The following script is sufficient for teaching you how to do it:

> *Closing your eyes and noticing where your body is touching the surfaces beneath you. Feeling the floor beneath your feet* (or "foot" if legs are crossed, better if both are on the floor), *the couch beneath your legs*

and seat, and the cushion behind you. Visualizing, imagining, that the surfaces beneath you are like sponges that instead of absorbing water, absorb tension from your body. Making no effort to relax, instead just feeling your tension being absorbed by the surfaces beneath you (pause). *Allowing gravity to help to drain the tension from your body* (pause). *Allowing your breathing to help so that each time you breathe out, you're feeling a little more relaxed.*

Four-muscle group recall is the final step of PR (Bernstein & Borkovec, 1973). Whether or not you have done PR, the sponge, or tin man-to-scarecrow with your client, ask your client how their muscles feel when they are deeply relaxed. In particular, ask them if they notice a difference in the perception of weight, explaining that most people feel as if their limbs in particular, feel heavy or light and floaty, or a combination of both. After teaching PR to hundreds of clients, I have never seen someone who doesn't notice a difference in weight perception after PR. Once they feel this difference in weight perception and other feelings such as loose, like jelly, or released, they can "recall," or remember, these feelings after having practiced progressive relaxation, the sponge, or "tin man to scarecrow."

Recall is useful when an individual is tired and doesn't really want to tense first. It's

Strategy #30: Recall

particularly useful in waiting rooms, meetings, airplanes, or in any situation in which there is an opportunity to relax, in which the person is held "captive" and it would be odd for them to tense. Because in many of these places one's head and neck cannot be supported and the chair may be uncomfortable, I do not ask the person to "get comfortable" before beginning this procedure. However, I do ask that they close their eyes.

The first step is to have them notice the tension that they are feeling in their hands and arms. I will even ask them to increase the tension without actually tightening the muscles. As with PR, I use continuous patter on this for 5-10 seconds and then ask them to recall the feelings of relaxation for 30-40 seconds. So, for instance, if the individual states that their muscles feel heavy and like jelly after getting deeply relaxed, my patter might be as follows:

Closing your eyes and noticing the tension in your hands and arms. Even allowing that tension to increase without actually tightening those muscles. Feel the tension. (pause) *Recalling how those muscles feel when they're most deeply relaxed* (pause) *heavy like jelly. Just enjoying how your arms and legs feel. Making no effort to relax; just remembering how those muscles feel when they are released and heavy like jelly.*

Then repeat this same idea with the following three groups: 1. face and neck 2. torso and 3. legs and feet. Of course this procedure can be done with more or fewer muscle groups and one can skip or shorten the portion of noticing tension.

MINDFULNESS

Since Jon Kabat-Zinn (1990) helped to westernize mindfulness and Marsha Linehan (1993) began using it as part of dialectical behavior therapy, mindfulness has become

> Strategy #31: Mindful observation of the senses to be in the moment.

increasingly popular as a part of stress and anxiety management. Think of the utility of mindfulness as being two-fold: 1) a means to relax by being in the moment to focus on ones senses and 2) observation and acceptance as a way to reduce emotional pain, whether it's anxiety or another emotion. This chapter will address the former. See Chapter 4 for the latter.

Focusing on the moment by focusing on one's senses is quite simple. The client observes what they hear, see, feel, and sometimes what they smell and taste. At this very moment as I write this, I am fortunate enough to be on a covered deck during a thunderstorm after having eaten some fresh cherries about 20 minutes ago. I can continue to write, but still enjoy the sounds of the thunder and the rain. Earlier, I could hear the wind rustling the trees, but the storm is waning. I can see flashes of lightning in my periphery now and then and occasionally look up to see the rain and the trees as I'm in a wooded area. I still enjoy a subtle flavor of the cherries and smell the effect of the rain.

In my office I have a fountain, and we have white noise in the vents. I also have a rather large and interesting piece of art across

> Strategy #32: Mindful like a baby.

from where clients usually sit and sometimes burn a scented candle. I typically start with eyes closed and eventually have them open their eyes. I experiment by having them focus on all of their available senses (smell and taste often are not present) and then whittling down to their two favorites, then to one sense. All the while accepting that they will notice their other senses in the background. Then I have them notice which is better, focusing on one sense, two senses, or allowing their mind to float freely among their senses. I encourage them to focus on their senses "like a baby would, a baby who can see, hear, feel, smell, and taste, but she ("he" if I'm with a male) doesn't have words for her experiences. Noticing the raw sensations."

Because we are thinkers and have thousands of thoughts per hour, teach people to expect that thoughts from the past and future will interfere with their mindfulness of the moment. The goal is not to eliminate thoughts when relaxing, rather to reduce them. However, I employ a *game* of thought labeling to use when people are struggling with too many thoughts. If the difficulty of staying in the moment is such that people are rapidly moving back and forth between the future and the present or the past and the present or more time is spent worrying, the labeling game is indicated. Thought labeling employs the following steps:

1. Focusing on your senses as a baby would.
2. When thoughts interfere, taste the thought and then gently shifting to . . . focusing on your senses.
3. When you find that you are struggling to be in the moment ... label your experiences.
4. When solidly in the present go back to focusing on your senses as a baby would.
5. Repeat steps 4-6 as needed.

For most clients I present this as a game. The goal is to be aware when thoughts are interfering and to be able to gently shift attention to the moment, rather than struggling with the thoughts or trying to eliminate them. The following is a script for the labeling game when taking a walk with your client.

> **Strategy #33: Mindful Labeling Game**

> *Noticing the wind. Feeling it on your body, hearing it in your ear and moving the leaves. Seeing the wind moving trees and plants.* (pause) *Noticing how the landscape is changing as we move forward, noticing the colors, shapes, textures, shadows.* (pause) *Hearing and feeling your shoes on the pavement as you move forward.* (pause) *Noticing if you can smell anything* (or if there is an obvious smell ... *noticing the smell of ...). Feeling the warmth of the sun (if applicable) and as we move under the shade of the trees, feeling the difference.* (pause) *We are thinkers, so thoughts will interfere with your enjoyment of the moment. When they do, accepting those thoughts, tasting the thought,*

and then gently moving your mind back to your senses. (pause) *Noticing what you hear,* (brief pause) *see,* (brief pause) *feel,*

| Strategy #34: Mindfulness Walk |

(brief pause) and smell. Noticing these senses as a baby would. A baby who can see, hear, feel, and smell, but doesn't have words for her experiences. Just noticing the raw sensations. (pause) *If you find that your thoughts are interfering more than you'd like and you are having difficulty being mostly in the present, begin to label your experiences in the moment. For instance if I were to label my experiences . . . hearing birds, lamppost, smelling the grass, white clouds, blue sky, hearing a plane, seeing a plane, dog barking, feeling my legs moving, pavement beneath my feet. When you feel solidly in the present, letting go of the labels and going back to focusing on your senses as a baby would.*

It can be particularly useful to demonstrate mindfulness during a walk. However, respecting your clients' privacy is important. So before you take a walk explain to your client that either of you might see someone you know while on this walk and that it might be uncomfortable for them. Usually people say it's not a problem, but make it clear that they can forgo the mindful walk.

BREATHING

"Just take a deep breath" is the frequent refrain we hear from therapists, clients, and others as advice on how to relax. While there is some

| Strategy #35: Diaphragmatic breathing |

validity to this, the phrase can be misleading. Many misperceive it as a directive to take a big breath. Taking a big breath is unnatural and can even be stressful. If taking a big breath works, it's likely a distraction, a placebo, or a false sense of control. Likewise, the various methods such as counting to 10 while breathing in and out, or counting to 10 breathing in, to 5 breathing out, and to 5 during the pause are not really healthful unless one is slowing their breathing from a state of hyperventilation.

Shallow breathing can cause hyperventilation, because the lungs can only absorb oxygen into the blood stream through the bottom of the lungs. The top of the lungs are completely void of alveoli, tiny grape-like structures that are the only avenue for allowing oxygen to be transferred into the blood stream. Alveoli, found exclusively in the bottom of the lungs, are best utilized when we breathe using the diaphragm to expand the lungs. The diaphragm is a muscle that is attached to the bottom of the lungs. When we breathe in properly our diaphragms, which are arch-shaped when at rest, flatten to expand the lungs thereby allowing air to flow freely into the bottom of the lungs where the alveoli can absorb oxygen into them (see diagram). Therefore, when "deep breathing" involves allowing the air we breathe in to reach "deep" into the bottom of the lungs, it can help an individual to feel more relaxed.

To the contrary, when relying on breathing from the top of the lungs in a shallow manner, it takes many more breaths for enough oxygen to get into the blood stream. The stress this causes is two-fold. First, the labored breathing itself causes tension in the respiratory muscles that can lead to chest discomfort and even pain. Second, too much carbon dioxide is expelled, leading to hyperventilation. When carbon dioxide levels get too low, the oxygen binds more to blood, decreasing its delivery to the tissues. Because low carbon dioxide levels also cause the blood vessels to constrict, there are two ways that our organs do not get sufficient oxygen. For the most part, we are breathing in enough oxygen. However, the narrowed blood vessels combined with increased oxygen binding to the blood, restricts the amount of oxygen our organs receive. One of those organs is the brain. It reacts to the lower levels of oxygen it's receiving by causing the feeling of not getting enough air. In turn, this leads to increased respiration which only exacerbates the problem of feeling breathless because more and more carbon-dioxide is being expelled. As the feeling of breathlessness increases, so does the fear of panic, leading to a self-fulfilling prophecy as the sympathetic nervous system response often cascades into a full-blown panic attack. Breathing retraining is teaching the client to right this problem by explaining the physiology and rationale while teaching them to breathe more effectively.

Antony (2000) questions the utility of breathing retraining after presenting a review of studies that indicate that it is minimally effective and at least one study showing that it adds nothing to CBT (Schmidt et al., 2000). He cites research that it is likely only helpful because it offers a distraction and a sense of control, two elements that are contraindicated when doing exposures. Schmidt et al. (2000) also reports that trends in their data "suggest introduction of breathing retraining may adversely affect patients, leading to less complete recovery and greater risk for relapse." If clients rely too heavily on diaphragmatic breathing it may negatively reinforce anxiety and actually interfere with desensitization when doing exposure therapy and when combating panic outside of therapy. In addition, some clients become hyper-aware of their breathing such that *trying to breathe the right way* can often contribute to anxiety.

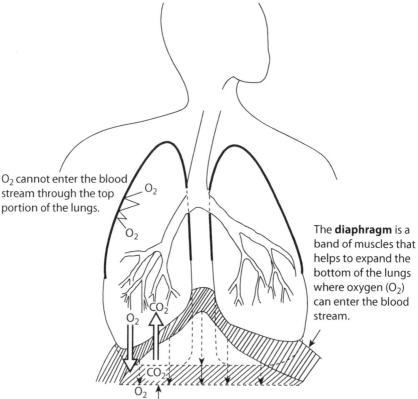

O_2 cannot enter the blood stream through the top portion of the lungs.

The **diaphragm** is a band of muscles that helps to expand the bottom of the lungs where oxygen (O_2) can enter the blood stream.

When too much carbon dioxide (CO_2) leaves the blood stream the blood vessels narrow and O_2 clings to the blood. The result is that the organs get less O_2, including the brain. The brain causes you to feel out of breath so that you will take in more O_2 which only releases more CO_2 making you feel even more out of breath. This is **hyperventilation**.

When the diaphragm is not utilized to breathe, chest breathing occurs. Chest breathing can cause **hyperventilation**.

I concur that it is best to use discretion when considering teaching diaphragmatic breathing. Because exposure-based treatments and cognitive therapy appear to be more effective and diaphragmatic breathing may negatively reinforce anxiety in some cases, it is *often* best to avoid utilizing breathing strategies (See Chapter 8 for a detailed explanation of negative reinforcement). Nonetheless, I believe it is a good practice when interoceptive and other forms of exposure are contraindicated, ineffective, or refused by the client. I also believe it can be particularly useful when shallow breathing is observed, and the client hyperventilates during many of their panic attacks. In fact, when hyperventilation plays a significant role in panic, diaphragmatic breathing has been shown to be effective (Garssen, Buikhuisen, & van Dyke, 1996). Recent research found that individuals suffering from "out-of-the-blue" panic attacks are chronically hyperventilating; (Mueret et. al, 2011) lending additional support to the use of diaphragmatic breathing in at least some cases.

Furthermore, if clients are taught to move toward relaxation rather than away from anxiety and use diaphragmatic breathing as a means to prevent panic instead of escape panic, there is less concern for negative reinforcement. Similarly, if mindful breathing is utilized wherein clients simply observe their breathing, rather than being taught to breathe in the "right way," there may also be less potential for escape.

When deciding that diaphragmatic breathing is an option, observe clients breathing first. Notice how they are breathing both

> Strategy #36: Mindful Breathing

when they complain of being anxious and when they are relaxed during guided meditation or relaxation. Also notice whether their breathing changes when drawing their attention to it during mindful breathing (see below). After observing their breathing while they are relaxed, it's a win-win. If their breathing is shallow even when relaxed then your rationale is that you have good news:

> *I noticed that even when you're relaxed your breathing is very shallow. In other words you're using only the top portion of your lungs to breathe and it's certainly contributing to your anxiety. This is good news because you can learn to breathe in a more healthful way that is likely to decrease your anxiety.*

If they are breathing well when relaxed then your rationale is also that you have good news:

*I noticed that when you're relaxed your breathing looks great. Many
people use only the top portion of their lungs to breathe and even when
relaxed can't seem to breathe into the bottom of their lungs as we'd like
to see. It's likely that your breathing changes when you are anxious.
So maintaining healthy breathing is likely to help you prevent having
panic attacks in the future.*

Provide a rationale explaining the aforementioned pulmonary physiology. Then explain that breathing from the diaphragm is a natural process that many of us somehow unlearn. Perhaps for at least some people, this is due to trying to appear thinner by holding in the stomach, thereby forcing shallow breathing. Regardless of the reason, we see proof that breathing from the stomach is natural by observing babies and children who always breathe from their diaphragms.

It is useful to master this skill yourself in order to demonstrate it properly to your clients. Place one hand on your belly and one hand on your chest. Sitting sideways when demonstrating is best so that clients can observe how the hand on your chest will remain stationary while the hand on your stomach will move as you breathe in. Ask your client to place one hand on their belly and one hand on their chest and mimic what you are doing, keeping their upper hand relatively still while allowing the air to go deep into the lungs, moving their stomach. When people have difficulty with this process there are strategies that can help people to be able to breathe effectively:

1. "Just *allowing* the air to travel to the bottom of your lungs as you allow your belly to expand."

2. "Letting go of trying to breathe in any particular way. Simply push out your stomach and allow it to relax. Keep repeating this. Now allowing your belly to expand as you breathe in."

3. Ask your client to blow through a regular sized straw.

4. "Think of expanding your sides as you breathe in."

5. Have them lie on their back or just lean back at about a 45 degree angle or lower. Get two books and have them put one on their stomach and one on their chest. "As you breathe in, keep the top book still while allowing the bottom book to move."

6. People can best feel their diaphragms moving by lying on their stomachs. If your office furniture allows, have your client lie on their stomach and feel their diaphragm working.

Whether or not you decide to utilize diaphragmatic breathing, you can have your clients engage in mindful breathing. Here is a sample script for mindful breathing:

> *Making no effort to breathe in any certain way, instead just observing your breathing* (pause) *following your breathing* (pause). *As you begin focusing on your nose, noticing that as you breathe in the air feels cool and as you breathe out the air feels warmer. Feeling the cool air expanding your lungs as you inhale and noticing the warmer air escaping through your nose as your lungs relax. Noticing that just after you breathe out your body is still before you breathe in. Enjoying that quiet pause. Noticing how still and relaxed your body is between breaths.*

In addition, you can add relaxing words to breathing. I recommend using one syllable each for inhalation/exhalation, and just enjoying the quiet pause. Alternatively use a

> **Strategy #37: Add relaxing words to mindful breathing.**

syllable for the quiet pause too. So, for instance, thinking the word *cool* as you breathe in, the word *warm* as you breathe out and just enjoying the quiet pause between breaths. Or you can use *letting go*. "*Let*" as you breathe in "*-ting*" as you breathe out and "*go*" during the quiet pause.

Clients particularly like counting backwards during the quiet pause. "Thinking *peace* as you breathe in, *calm* as you breathe out, and on the next quiet pause thinking the number five. On the following quiet pause the number *four*. Using one lower number for each quiet pause, counting all the way down to zero. When you get to zero taking one more breath and then opening your eyes." Instead of asking them to open their eyes you can continue with other forms of relaxation. So, for instance, "when you get to zero taking one more breath and then gently shifting your attention to the surfaces beneath you."

Add imagery to breathing to induce deeper relaxation. Have your client visualize themselves breathing in a cool color, like blue

> **Strategy #38: Add color imagery to breathing.**

or aqua, fresh-clear oxygenated air, or another color that they find relaxing. As they exhale, "breathing out a warm color like red, yellow, or orange." Alternatively ask them to visualize what color their anxiety feels like in their chest or stomach and have them visualize gently breathing out that color. Allowing the anxiety color to slowly be released rather than trying to push it out.

Nearly everyone enjoys being at the beach and finds the sound of the ocean relaxing. When it's quiet, a great imagery is to focus on the sound of breathing and imagine that it is the sound of the ocean:

> Strategy #39: Combine breathing with imagery of the beach.

Gently closing your eyes and beginning focusing on your breathing. Noticing that the sound of your breathing sounds very much like waves on the ocean. As you breathe in it sounds as if the waves are rolling in and as you breathe out it's like the ebb is falling back into the ocean. After the waves fall back into the ocean there's a quiet pause before the next wave comes in. Noticing how relaxing it is to be at one with the ocean. Enjoying that your breathing and the ocean feel at one. Beginning to visualize the waves, if you haven't already. As the waves are rolling in, smelling the fresh salt air, sunscreen, or any other smell you associate with the ocean. Imagining feeling the wind and a mist off of the ocean. Noticing what time of day it is and whether you can feel the sun. Imagining the taste and temperature of a cool drink.

IMAGERY

You have just read about how to use imagery in managing muscle tension and how to combine it with mindful breathing. Many therapists use imagery as a form of relaxation. Perhaps the most popular is to have a client imagine that they are in a beautiful place where they have been before, a place they've seen in movies or photos, or an imaginary place. While leading the imagery, the therapist guides the client to notice most, if not all, of the five senses.

Imagery can also be used to help individuals manage stress in a way that begins by imagining the stress in a different way and slowly reducing it. As previously discussed, catching anxiety early and preventing it is the crux of managing worry and it is also useful in panic. However, when anxiety is high the following imagery strategies can be helpful.

Running With Thoughts

When thoughts are racing, one can think of their worries as racing while they are running. Guide your clients to visualize themselves

> Strategy #40: Sprinting to Walking with Thoughts

sprinting while engaging in their "racing" thoughts. It is helpful to write down your clients' racing thoughts first and then say them very rapidly as you have them visualize themselves sprinting. Then have them visual-

> Strategy #41: Merry-go-round with thoughts.

ize themselves running as you slow the script of the thoughts a bit. Next jog with the thoughts, followed by walking, while you talk at a normal pace. You can then follow it with walking slowly, then stopping and sitting. Instead of saying the thoughts, you can simply instruct your client to think the thoughts while slowing them as their stride slows.

Similar to the running thoughts, you can use the imagery of a child's merry-go-round. The kind you find in your local park that is propelled by putting one's foot on the merry-go-round and using the other foot to increase the speed. Imagining running around in circles, as worry often feels, and then hopping on and letting the worry slow along with the visual of the merry-go-round slowing.

The record player strategy employs both speed and volume of the thoughts. It is useful for clients who remember the old time record

> Strategy #42: Record Player

players with three speeds (or even four speeds for very elderly clients). Again, writing down the "spinning" worry helps to demonstrate this to your client. Begin by having them visualize their worries on a 45 rpm record on a 3-speed record player. Say their worries fast and loud as they imagine their worries being playing at 78rpm at full volume. Then have them imagine turning down the volume as you speak in a normal tone of voice. Next ask them to visualize turning down the record player to 45 rpm as you speak at a normal rate. Finally, lower the speed and volume, talking slowly and quietly before turning the volume all the way down until it turns off. Once it is off, shifting to mindfulness or another relaxation strategy before asking the client to open his or her eyes.

When people have many things on their minds there is some nice imagery that can be used to allow them to embrace worries and gently let go of them. For the following imageries, rather than explain them, it is best for me to provide the scripts:

The Mind Sink:

> *Visualizing your worries are in a sink inside of your head. You can visualize them*

> Strategy #43: Mind Sink

as words like alphabet soup in this sink, but with words or sentences instead of just letters. There is a plug in the bottom of the sink such that the words are staying in your mind sink. Taking a few moments to observe these thoughts in your mind sink. (pause) *Visualizing now that you are pulling out the plug. Allowing the thoughts to drain out of the sink, out of your mind. Gently pouring a large glass of water in the sink to help clear out the thoughts if you'd like.*

Balloons:

Visualizing that you are outdoors. This can be in your backyard, the park, or anywhere else outside. Imagining that you are holding a handful of helium balloons. Each balloon represents a different one of your tasks. Feeling a breeze on the back of your body. As you're holding this handful of balloons, thinking about what you are going to be doing after the session. (pause) *Taking the balloon that represents what you are doing next into your free hand. If the thing you're doing next is something you are looking forward to doing, make the balloon your favorite color. Letting go of the handful of balloons, watching them climb higher in the sky from the helium as the wind moves them farther and farther away. Seeing the balloons appearing smaller and smaller in your field of vision* (pause), *soon they are just a few little dots in the sky until they completely disappear. Focusing on your next event. If the balloon you're still holding is a task or worry, you're here in your session now such that it is best to focus on the moment by letting go of this last balloon too. Watching it float up into the sky and drifting further away.* (pause) *Seeing it get smaller and smaller until it's just a dot in the sky before it disappears completely. When it disappears, focusing your attention on the moment, noticing the surfaces beneath you* (and so forth).

> Strategy #44: Balloons

Boat and Dock:

Visualizing that you are standing on a dock on a large creek or small river with several boxes. Each box represents a different worry or item on your "to-do" list. There is a boat or a raft tied to the dock. Think about which box represents what you would like to do after leaving the appointment today. Put that box in the boat, get in the boat, untie it, allowing you to float downstream. Feeling the dock getting farther and farther behind you as you become more and more

> Strategy #45: Boat and dock

aware of the water, trees, and sky. Noticing all that you see, hear, feel, and smell as your troubles fall farther in the distance. Given that you are just enjoying the boat ride now, if you'd like, you can throw or push your box ashore and just continue to enjoy nature. Noticing everything you hear, see, feel, and smell as you float downstream.

CHAPTER SIX

Better but Believable Thoughts

Most therapists practice cognitive therapy on some level, even if it is just offering a different perspective during the course of talk therapy. Perhaps the earliest book on changing thoughts to improve mental health was *The Power of Positive Thinking* written by a minister by the name of Norman Vincent Peale (1952). The most popular book on cognitive therapy is *Feeling Good: The New Mood Therapy* by David Burns (1980). But many other famous mental health care professionals have published books on cognitive therapy. The early famous cognitive therapists are Aaron Beck (1967) and Albert Ellis (1961) whose work gained the respect of mental health care professionals in the early 1960's. One treatment element that all Beck, Ellis, and Burns have in common is identifying various thought styles in which clients typically engage such as *catastrophizing, filtering, shoulds,* and *mind-reading* and collaborating with the client to replace them with alternative positive thoughts. These strategies have proven to be effective for generalized anxiety disorder (e.g., Borkovec, Newman, Pincus, & Lytle, 2002) and panic disorder (e.g., Beck, Sokol, Clark, Berchick, & Wright, 1992).

One problem with these methods of cognitive therapy is that they are time-consuming and complex. First the client is asked to identify the anxiety-producing thought and then they are expected to figure out from a list of ten to fifteen maladaptive thought styles, the thought style(s) in which they are engaging. Next the client is expected to look at a list of suggestions on how to combat each of those maladaptive thought styles. From these instructions they are to construct a new thought that is more positive. The result is that this laborious process can sometimes increase stress, or the time commitment involved can cause a person to abandon his or her efforts or only use it after anxiety or depression has spiraled to a higher level.

Another potential problem in using cognitive therapy to treat clients with anxiety issues is the commonly used suggestion to simply "think positive." The goal is often to think the most positive thought they can. The bottom line is that if the person doesn't really believe that the thought is true, it's going to be useless. It's better to think of a neutral thought that is better than the feared thought – even if it isn't particularly positive. In summary, another pitfall of delivering cognitive-behavioral therapy in working with anxious clients is making cognitive therapy too complex or too unrealistically positive to the point of being unbelievable.

In an effort to eradicate both of these problems, Tom Borkovec simplified cognitive therapy for worriers into a Socratic approach to it. He suggested that worriers ask themselves: "What is something equally true or *more* true that is less anxiety-producing?" The idea is that most worries are very negative and often reflect the worst-case scenario. Therefore, there is almost always a thought that is more positive, less anxiety-producing, and yet true.

Given that stress often involves something that is anger-producing, frustrating, or irritating, and not just anxiety-producing, one could substitute any of these phrases for the phrase *anxiety-producing*. For example, when your client is frustrated they could ask themself, "What is something equally true, or more true, that is less frustrating?"

Although much simpler than the aforementioned process, some people *still* find the question, "what is something equally true, or

> Strategy #46: B³s (Better-But-Believable thoughts)

more true, but less _____ producing?" a bit cumbersome. Therefore, I have simplified this concept even further. The new Socratic question to ask oneself when feeling stressed is: "What is better-but-believable?" or for short, "B³": **B**etter-**B**ut-**B**elievable. A similar way to think of this type of thinking is that when we are worried we are wearing poop-colored glasses, and we see everything as being worse than reality. With B³s, instead of replacing the poop-colored glasses with rose-colored glasses, we replace them with clear glasses. We see reality; we see truth. In addition, we can choose to look at the more positive side of reality.

PRACTICING B³S

The example I like to use to illustrate B³s is that of a mother named Amanda who is worried about her son. He has asked if he can ride his bike with friends. She is afraid he will get hurt or even killed riding his bike. Her worry is, "I am so afraid he's going to get hurt or, even worse, be maimed, paralyzed, or killed."

In this situation, thinking the most positive thought "I'm sure he'll be fine" will not work, because it is not believable. Amanda's fear is based on the reality that children get hurt on their bikes every day and in rare instances the results tragic. She knows that he could get hurt. She may find herself reflecting on experiences in which she, her son, or someone close to her was hurt in an accident, even if it wasn't on a bike. She might be wrought with images of a news story about a kid who was killed on his bike. However, the reality is also that he is very unlikely to get hurt that day but rather very likely to be safe. In addition, most of the time when kids get hurt on their bikes it is an injury from which they will completely recover, such as a skinned knee. Nonetheless, fear is fueled by the fact that there is never a guarantee of safety. Amanda could use problem solving to improve the likelihood he'll be safe (e.g., have him wear a helmet, teach him safety, have the bike checked periodically), but unless she prohibits him from riding his bike, there is no way to guarantee that he won't get hurt on his bike. Furthermore, telling him "no" would likely create a host of other stressors. Her focusing on this fear is not only useless, it's also unduly stressful. If this were your client, the best way to get the most B^3s and improve the likelihood of finding something very useful, is to independently make a list of B^3s and then compile the lists. Before you read on, jot down four to five B^3s that might help this woman to feel less stressed and less worried. If you have a pen or pencil handy, do that in the space below. Otherwise, make a mental list.

> **Strategy #47:**
> **Brainstorm B^3s**

1.

2.

3.

4.

5.

Are all of your B^3s related to safety? If so, try to think outside the box. Try to come up with at least three thoughts that are better than "what if he gets hurt" but that are not about safety.

Below is my list.

1. *I cannot protect him from everything; I could keep him inside and he could get hurt in here too.*

2. *Millions of kids ride their bikes safely every day.*

3. *Millions of people ride their bikes safely throughout their lifetime.*

4. *There is at least a 95 percent chance that he will be fine.*

5. *If he does get hurt, it will likely be something from which he will recover, like a skinned/bruised knee.*

6. *Getting skinned up and bruised is part of being a child. It's to be expected from time to time.*

7. *If he does skin his knee or elbow, he might be a little more careful in the future.*

8. *He's wearing a helmet.*

9. *There is safety in numbers.*

10. *I complain that he plays video games too much; this is good that he's getting out of the house.*

11. *He will socialize and bond with his friends.*

12. *If I don't let him go, his friends might make fun of him.*

13. *He'll feel less a part of the group if I don't let him go.*

14. *He will be angry and sad if I don't let him go. While I know that it's wrong to allow him to do things because he will be angry with me, I know that I tend to be overprotective. It would be unreasonable for me to ask him not to ride his bike, a normal activity that boys his age do.*

15. *If I don't let him go, he'll ask why. When I tell him that I'm afraid he'll get hurt, he might become overly fearful. Or worse, he may retaliate and take bigger risks.*

16. *He will probably have a lot more fun riding bikes than whatever else he'd do.*

17. *He will get a chance to improve his gross motor skills.*

18. *Those motor skills can help him to improve his confidence in sports, and that is likely to transfer to other parts of his life.*

19. *Getting exercise is great for his physical health.*

20. *Getting exercise helps his emotional health as well.*

21. *He'll probably be more relaxed this evening because of the exercise.*

22. *He'll burn less electricity than if he stayed home and played video games.*

23. *He won't mess up the house while he's outside riding his bike.*

24. *I'll have more peace without him here.*

Notice that less than half of the thoughts listed here are about safety. I mentioned the positive qualities of socializing, getting exercise, having fun, and improving his motor skills and thereby improving his confidence. I also recognized that he would be justifiably angry and sad if she tried to stop him.

In addition, I thought about his becoming fearful about riding his bike as well as the possibility that he could retaliate by taking more risks to try to prove to her that she can't control him. I considered how good things can come out of "bad" things such that if he sustained a minor injury it may result in his being more careful, thereby helping to prevent something catastrophic. Finally, I considered the advantages for Amanda – that he can't mess up the house while riding his bike and she will have more peace.

A common mistake in teaching cognitive therapy is to continue to focus on the negative in the construction of the more positive thought. For instance, if you were to say to your client, "It is highly unlikely that he will get seriously hurt," or "There is less than a one percent chance that he will sustain a serious injury," they are still focusing on the possibility of his getting hurt. When you do this, your clients are likely to focus on "seriously hurt" or "sustain a serious injury" rather than that it's unlikely to happen. She might even start to visualize him in the emergency room in pain or worse yet at his funeral.

Therefore when coming up with B^3s, word them in a positive manner with the focus on being fine rather than a grave outcome being unlikely. So for instance, instead of the aforementioned statements: "It is likely he'll

> Strategy #48: Indicate the likelihood of the positive outcome vs. the negative one

come in the door fine with a big smile on his face." or "There's a better than 99 percent chance he'll be completely fine or just skin a knee or elbow." To add to the B^3s' effect encourage your client to visualize the positive, realistic outcome.

Try this exercise. Pretend that you are in this situation and you are afraid that your son (even if you don't have a young son) will get hurt or killed on his bike. Say this out loud if you are somewhere private, or just think it and feel it: "There is greater than a 95 percent chance that he will ride safely." Notice how this feels. Now say, "There is less than a five percent chance that he will get hurt." Most people report that the former feels better.

Once the two of you have constructed a list of B^3s, ask your client to rate on a 0-10 scale (or similar scale) how helpful they feel each B^3 will be when they begin to worry about the topic. Either write them in the margin or ask them to write the rating in the margin. Your goal is then to narrow the list down to the top two to four B^3s by choosing the statements with the highest ratings.

In some cases it will be easy to choose the top-rated B^3s. However, sometimes it's more challenging. If there are many B^3s with the same rating such that you come up with more than four, look for B^3s that are similar enough as to be almost redundant and eliminate the one(s) that seem less helpful.

Alternatively, you can combine them to make one B^3. So for instance, let's say that in the situation above Amanda had four B^{3s} rated as a "7" and one rating of an "8," "getting exercise is great for his physical health." If one of the B^3s that is rated a "7" is "getting exercise is great for his emotional health" you could combine those two into one statement "getting exercise is great for his mental and physical health." Let's say that two of the other "7's" on her list were "He will socialize and bond with his friends" and "If I don't let him go his friends might make fun of him." In this case, the items are similar enough to eliminate the negative statement and choose "He will socialize and bond with his friends" because it is more positive.

I suggest eliminating less helpful B^3s to arrive at a short list of B^3s, because it is more simple and less cumbersome for the client. You want to avoid overwhelming a client who is already anxious. There are exceptions to the rule. One is if there are several highly ranked B^3s that are helpful in very different ways. For example, let's say that the following statements for Amanda in the example above were all rated a "7" or an "8":

1. Millions of kids ride their bikes safely every day.
2. I complain that he plays video games too much; this is good that he's getting out of the house.
3. He will socialize and bond with his friends.
4. He will probably have a lot more fun riding bikes than whatever else he'd do.
5. I'll have more peace without him here.
6. If I don't let him go, he'll ask why. When I tell him that I'm afraid he'll get hurt, he might become overly fearful. Or worse, he may retaliate and take bigger risks.
7. Getting exercise is great for his physical health.

All of these B^3s are dissimilar. In this case, selecting more than four items may be beneficial. There may be other reasons that a client will want to choose several B^3s. Weighing the benefits of having a more complete list versus feeling overwhelmed by having too many items is something you can discuss with your client on an individual basis.

After you and your client have come up with the best B^3 s, it is useful to have them say aloud their initial anxious, or otherwise upsetting, thought. Ask them to say it again and notice how it feels. Then ask them to say aloud the best B^{3s} while noticing how they feel. It can also be helpful to have them rate the believability of their B³s. These thoughts are likely to be even more believable if you encourage your client to combine them with relaxation. If

Strategy #49: Improve believability of B³s by adding relaxation.

believability ratings are low, it can be very useful to use relaxation or meditation in the session and, once they are relaxed, say the B³s aloud and re-rate their believability. Similarly, using relaxation before generating a list of B³s may be helpful.

Suggest that clients write their top B³s on a note card or enter the short list into their smartphone or tablet. You might suggest that they memorize these thoughts. Remind them to use these thoughts early in the worry spiral. In addition, when they are using B³s on their own, suggest that they have a friend or family member help develop their list, particularly if they aren't happy with any of their own B³s or they seem to have difficulty thinking flexibly.

Going through the trouble of generating a long list each time one has a negative thought may defeat the purpose of the simplicity of B³s. Therefore, in most situations it is sufficient for clients to simply think about a few B³s and choose one or two. It is good to use the preceding method as a didactic tool to demonstrate the usefulness of B³s and "get their creative juices flowing." It is also very useful to use the longer method when your client has had difficulty letting go of an intense worry or if a worry reoccurs over the course of weeks. For example the detailed B³ method would be appropriate if Amanda's son rode his bike with his friends frequently, and she continually struggled with worrying about him time and time again. It may also be helpful for a more acute situation that is causing a great deal of distress. However, for practical reasons, most of the time your client will be using B³s, they will quickly think of just a handful of B³s, usually without stopping their flow of activity. Then they will pick one or two, maybe three, B³s to think when the negative thought begins to surface.

Cognitive therapy in combination with catching the spiral early has been shown to be as effective as applied relaxation and self-control desensitization in the treatment of GAD (Borkovec et. al, 2002). Relaxation strategies *may* be best however, because relaxation is the same regardless of the situation or worry, whereas cognitive therapy varies depending upon the nature of the worry. Nonetheless, even after a two-year follow up, individuals who learned cognitive therapy only fared as well as those receiving relaxation therapy and a combination of both treatments. Due to individual differences, I teach both with all worried clients.

Cognitive therapy has been shown to be very effective in the treatment of panic disorder in at least one study (Beck et. al, 1992) with 79% to 82% (the former was in a control group before receiving cognitive therapy) of clients remaining panic-free for a full year. The advantage to cognitive therapy is that it is a kinder, gentler approach to exposure therapies (See Chapters 9 and 10). However, three meta-analyses found that exposure therapies or exposure combined with cognitive therapy were most effective (Westen & Morrison, 2001; Clum, Clum, & Surls, 1993; Gould, Otto, & Pollack, 1993). The other disadvantage to utilizing cognitive therapy in the treatment of panic is that the therapist and the client may use the positive thoughts in a way that negatively reinforces anxiety if not careful (See Chapter 8). I routinely see clients who respond well to exposure therapies after having failed with cognitive therapy and relaxation with other therapists or myself.

In summary, a common pitfall of practicing cognitive therapy is making it so complex that clients' compliance wanes. Another problem is generating very positive thoughts that are not believable. Better-but-believable thoughts, or the B^3 strategy is an alternative to applying cognitive therapy that rectifies these problems, making it more beneficial. B^3s make cognitive therapy simpler to utilize and more believable increasing the likelihood that clients will comply and therefore benefit from cognitive therapy. When using B^3s to treat panic disorder, be careful to avoid negatively reinforcing anxiety (See Chapter 8).

CHAPTER SEVEN

Wanting to be Free from Anxiety and Other Cognitive Therapy Tools

While B³s are very useful for reducing anxiety when clients are thinking negatively, a habit of thinking that deserves special attention is imperatives. Other cognitive therapists refer to them as "shoulds" and Albert Ellis referred to the habit of telling oneself that one "must do this" or "must do that" as "musterbation." This habit is easily spotted and observed behaviorally in the initial evaluation. Clients who are under a great deal of stress are often anxious because they place a great deal of pressure on themselves. You can hear this in their use of imperatives during your sessions. The following is a fictional example of someone who may come into your office.

> *"I've known for a long time that I **should** do something about my anxiety, but I've put it off because I **need to** watch my budget and I have so many other things I **have to** do that take time and money. I know I **need to** stop worrying so much, but I can't stop it. I **have to** get a handle on myself and chill out."*

The pressure is excessive because the client is thinking that they "need to" do this and feeling that they "should" do that. This habit can become so engrained that some people

Strategy #50: Identify client's use of imperatives.

think or say the words "I need to," "I have to," or "I should" well over two hundred times a day. I know this because I have actually counted during the first portion of some psychotherapy sessions to make a point of how frequently these stress-inducing words occur in their communication. Without extra help identifying it, most people are unaware of the amount of stress that "shoulding on themselves" creates. These imperatives come in the form of "should," "need to," "have to," "gotta" and less commonly in the 21st century, "must."

Point out to your clients that the word shoulders has the word "should" in it. Ask them to think about when their shoulders are tense. It's likely that much of that tension can be attributed to the "shoulds," "have to's," and "need to's" that many of us tend to think and say on a habitual basis.

Although there are a few exceptions, most people learned this habit from their parents. "You need to clean your room" or "You have to go to sleep" are common refrains. As a child, the consequences might have been such that your client felt like there was no choice. However, most people had a choice. Even though the consequences faced for not doing it might not be worth it, there was nearly always a choice to not do it and suffer the consequences. (However, one could certainly argue that if the parents were really abusive, the child had no choice but to conform, and is best addressed early in therapy.)

As a result of such parenting, as adults many people feel as though they have no choice when hearing people tell them that they "should" do something or that they "need" to do something. However, the bigger problem is usually the self-imposed "shoulds" that our clients habitually tell themselves.

If these imperatives were not learned from parents, it may have been from older siblings, teachers, coaches, and other adults who "*need*ed" or "*should*ed" on them. Even if they said it nicely, *should* and *need* are words that place a lot of pressure on an individual. Your client may have felt guilty as though they were irresponsible, a bad person, or a failure if they didn't do what they were told that they "needed" to do. Therefore, your clients usually did whatever they felt like they should do to keep from feeling guilty or like a failure. The result is that these habits were negatively reinforced. Negative reinforcement is often misunderstood even by mental health care professionals. In short, it is when a bad or uncomfortable thing is removed; the relief from this change reinforces, or increases, that behavior. In other words, some people prevented feeling, or were relieved of feeling guilt by giving into a "should." The thought of feeling the fear or guilt becomes stronger and stronger such that saying and "giving into" the should becomes a strong habit and often becomes automatic. Negative reinforcement is the primary reason why it's so hard to stop being emotionally ruled by both self-imposed "shoulds" as well as "shoulds" from others.

We feel what we think. Therefore if our clients *think* that they *need* to do something, they will feel like they need to do something, whether that is the reality or not. Typically it is not the reality. The reality is that about the only thing we absolutely need to do is to breathe, eat, sleep, and have shelter. But when our clients hear or think the word *need* they usually *feel* as if dire consequences await if they don't respond to the command. Many people use these imperatives as an unhealthy way to motivate themselves. They might mistakenly fear that without these words they will become complete failures, a couch potato, or end up living under a bridge.

The truth is that most of the time these words are actually counterproductive. They add tension and pressure, sometimes interfere with concentration, detract from enjoyment, and often zap energy. It appears that many people use these words to try to motivate themselves. While there may be times that this is effective, when it creates more anxiety this anxiety can interfere with productivity. Moderate amounts of arousal lead to the greatest productivity, while higher levels interfere with it (Yerkes & Dodson, 1908). It is also clear that worry interferes with problem solving (Dugas et al., 1995).

The habit of responding to these imperatives ends up becoming so problematic that often even the things that people usually enjoy cause stress. Even if the commitment is fun, or at least pleasant, the individual may be feeling as though it's a task or a chore and view it like an item on their "to-do" list. Instead of looking forward to it, they feel weighed down by that one additional thing on the list, waiting for their duty to be filled. They feel like they can't back out and would feel guilty if they did.

Here is an example of a dialogue I might have with a client. We'll call her Jeannie.

Jeannie: *I have so much to do. I have to go to the grocery store on the way home and then I need to call the electrician again, because our lights are still flickering, and then we have to go out to dinner tonight with some friends.*

Me: *You have to go to dinner with these friends?*

Jeannie: *Yeah, we already made the plans.*

Me: *Are these people you don't like?*

Jeannie: *Oh no, I like Brett and Mandy a lot. But I have to get dressed and ready and it would just be easier to stay at home.*

Me: *So, you don't have a lot of energy to think of getting ready and going out and keeping up conversation and so forth.*

Jeannie: *Yeah, at the end of the week I'm just so tired.*

Me: *Could you find out if they are available tomorrow night instead?*

Jeannie: *Well, they have kids, so I'm sure they already have a baby-sitter, and Saturdays aren't usually good for them because they go to church early on Sunday.*

Me: *Okay, so you've gone out with them on a Friday before.*

Jeannie: *Oh yeah, several times.*

Me: *How many times have you been sorry you went out with them and wished you would have stayed at home?*

Jeannie: *Well, you have a point there. Once I get out, I usually have a really good time with them. But one time I fell asleep in the movie we saw, because it was kind of slow and I am pretty tired on Fridays*

Me: *So, it sounds like you really do want to go and you will have fun and be glad.*

Jeannie: *Yeah!*

Me: *I'm wondering too if you could just ask not to see a movie on a Friday night and maybe even suggest a rush-hour show on a Saturday with dinner afterward? They can be back home early enough to get up for church and you will be more rested. It seems that they could be a little more flexible in the future. Do you agree?*

Jeannie: *Well, yeah, but they need to get up early for church.*

Me: *Is it more important that they're not tired for church than it is for you not to be tired when you're out with them?*

Jeannie: *Yeah, I see what you're saying, but they always vie for a Friday.*

Me: *But the truth is that you don't have to go out with them tonight, and you don't have to go out with them any other Friday night.*

Jeannie: *No, I disagree. I do need to go out with them tonight, because I made a commitment.*

Me: *I do think it's good to keep your commitments. But would you agree that you could cancel tonight and they would likely forgive you?*

Jeannie: *Well, yeah? But . . . (pause)*

Me: *I'm not suggesting that you cancel, because we already established that you will probably have fun, right?*

Jeannie: *Yeah!*

Me: *What is more accurate? Is it more accurate to say that you have to go tonight, or that you could cancel, but you want to go because you will probably have fun, you like to keep your commitments, and you will likely be glad that you went?*

Jeannie: *I guess I don't really have to go, but the better point is that I do want to. Yeah, that helps! Now I'm starting to look forward to it rather than seeing it as another chore.*

Me: *Great! Also, next time you go to make plans with Brett and Mandy, what if you were to explain to them that you get really tired on Fridays and think you would enjoy things more on Saturday and then suggest that you just make early plans on Saturday.*

Jeannie: *Hmmm. That might actually work.*

Me: *I'd like for you to try a little exercise. Okay?*

Jeannie: *Sure.*

Me: *Okay, say aloud, "I have to go out with Brett and Mandy tonight."*

Jeannie: *I have to go out with Brett and Mandy tonight.*

Me: *Now say aloud, "I want to go out with Brett and Mandy tonight."*

Jeannie: *I want to go out with Brett and Mandy tonight.*

Me: *Is that true?*

Jeannie: *Yes, it is!*

Me: *Which one feels better?*

Jeannie: *I feel like I have to, but more than that I really do want to. I think I'll also suggest an early Saturday next time.*

Me: *Fantastic! When you stop feeling like you "have to," you start to be more open to your options. Now let's talk about the other things that you mentioned that you have to do: call the electrician and go to the grocery store. Could you go to the grocery store tomorrow? And could you write yourself a note to call the electrician over the weekend or on Monday?*

Jeannie: *Oh, I hate going to the grocery store on a Saturday; it's so crowded.*

Me: *You want to go today because it isn't as crowded. You could go tomorrow, though. You could just pick up a few things and go next week. For about $10, you could pay for a grocery delivery service to avoid going altogether. Could your husband go?*

Jeannie: *He doesn't like to go, but you know the only things we really need are cereal and coffee, and I could get them at the convenience store and then I could relax for a few minutes before going out tonight.*

Me: *Okay, just be aware that you have options and when you are saying "need to" or "have to" or "should," consider to what extent it really is a "want to" or a "could."*

As you can see from this exchange, it is important to make an effort to ask your clients to be aware of their "shoulds," "need to's," and "have to's." First ask them what the consequences will be for not doing something. If your client still feels a need to do it, ask him or her how much flexibility is involved. For instance, it is typically pretty true that we all need to do laundry sometimes. However, there is some flexibility. If your client feels that they need to do it tonight, they probably could do it tomorrow. They could drop it off at the cleaners and have them do it. Perhaps they could hire someone to do it. Your client could wait until the weekend. Even if they are out of clean underwear, many people go without it sometimes. Even if they don't want to go without, it's certainly an option. If they really *want* to have clean underwear, they could even go buy new underwear. Sharing this scenario with your clients can add some humor. In a situation similar to this when none of these options are resonating, you conclude the scenario by saying something like this: "If you don't want to shop, or wait until tomorrow, or go to the cleaners, or wear dirty underwear, or go without underwear, then you really do *want* to do laundry because you *want* clean underwear.

The goal is to find a "want to" regardless of the situation (Abel, 2010). To further illustrate this point consider something that nobody wants to do: clean toilets. I don't know anyone who likes to clean toilets. If your toilet isn't dirty, visualize for a moment that you have a dirty toilet that bothers you when you use it. Now say out loud, "I need to clean the toilet." Notice how you feel. Notice your level of motivation to clean it.

Now visualize the toilet clean and say out loud, "I want the toilet to be clean." Notice the difference in how this feels. Also, notice whether your motivation changes. We are usually more motivated to do something positive than to do something negative. Your clients will likely be more motivated to have the toilets clean than they will be to want to clean the toilets.

Sometimes the key is to find a reason your client wants to do something, even if it is only to get it crossed off their list. Make certain they believe the statement. For instance, "I want my toilets to be clean" is significantly more believable than "I want to clean my toilets."

> **Strategy #51: Find the "want."**

A very common situation to which we can apply this concept is exercise. Many people "should on" themselves by thinking something like "I need to go to the gym." In this case a Socratic approach to "finding the want" can be best. Below are some of the questions you may ask your client.

What do you consider the advantages of exercise to be?

How will you feel if you don't go?

How many times when you have gone to the gym have you been sorry that you went?

Strategy #52: Use "the want" worksheet.

What is the likelihood that you will be glad that you went?

What are the reasons to not go?

Then you can use these responses to construct a "want to" statement. An example of such a statement is: I will be glad that I went to the gym because I will feel more relaxed, sleep better, and it is good for my mental and physical health. A similar process to arrive at this new perspective can be attained by using the follow worksheet:

Worksheet for Reframing Shoulds
(Abel, 2010)

What is the "should/need to" statement?
What will happen if I don't do it?
What is the "want to"?
When else could I do it or what are the alternatives?
What would make it more pleasant?
Will I be glad that I did it?
Reframed statement(s):

Applying the gym situation to the worksheet might look like this:

What is the "should/need to" statement?
I really need to go to the gym.
What will happen if I don't do it?
I'll be sorry that I skipped it and won't feel as good the rest of the day.
What is the "want to"?
I want to have that feeling I do after I leave the gym. I want to be healthy. I want to sleep well. I want to be in good shape.
When else could I do it or what are the alternatives?
I could go for a bike ride or a run. I could even go for a walk. In the future I could arrange to play racquetball with a friend or get into a soccer league.
What would make it more pleasant?
Taking some good tunes and a tasty sports drink.
Will I be glad that I did it?
Absolutely!
Reframed "want to" statement(s):
I will be glad that I went to the gym because I feel more relaxed, sleep better, and it is good for my mental and physical health. Therefore, I really do want to go to the gym.

Afterwards, have your client say the "should/need to" statement aloud and then say the reframed "want" statement.

Certainly there are more important and pressing responsibilities than a good workout that probably fall more into the category of "should" or "need to" than "want to." These would be responsibilities that if not done would cause dire consequences, such as picking up one's child from school or paying taxes. Nonetheless, these situations can still benefit from finding the "want to" as well as introducing some flexibility within the constraints of those responsibilities. Given the propensity of individuals with GAD to think in a myopic fashion, the idea of increasing flexibility is particularly important. This flexibility can be generated by starting a sentence with "I could." For instance, in the situation of the child (we will call him Ethan) *needing* to be picked up from school/daycare, we could generate the following "coulds" for the mother or father.

I could . . .

- call the school and arrange for a cab for Ethan (depending upon the city and age of the child).
- see if someone at daycare would be willing to bring Ethan to my office or house for extra pay.
- have him take public transportation (depending upon the city and age of the child).
- hire a trusted friend, babysitter, or family member to pick him up.
- arrange any of the above situations for the future.
- arrange any of the above situations on an "as-needed" basis. That is, have people on call.
- arrange the above situations on a regular basis for certain days (e.g., Mondays and Wednesdays).

Similarly with the tax situation. I could . . .

- avoid paying taxes and risk the consequences.
- estimate my taxes and file an extension.
- deal with the whole situation later and pay the fines.
- leave the country to avoid paying taxes.
- take on a new identity to avoid paying taxes.

Of course the last two options are completely unreasonable. However, introducing flexibility and humor to the situation can be helpful. When writing these unreasonable options, like "leave the country" or "risk the consequences" it can be helpful in eventually leading to a more solid "want to." This can be done by stating "I don't want to _____. Therefore, I really do want to _____." So for instance, I don't want to leave the country or take on a new identity, therefore, I want to pay my taxes.

Finally, thinking of the advantages to doing it can be helpful too. For example, I want to pay my taxes on time, because overall it will be less work, less money, and less hassle. I want to be a law-abiding citizen. Or, I want to pick up Ethan from school because he likes it, and I would miss seeing that big smile on his face when he sees me at school. In the end, one of the alternatives is desirable. If not, there is usually an option that is at least more desirable than the original statement containing the imperative. Chapters 11 and 12 about perfectionism and people pleasing explains more about how to break the pattern of shoulds for these specific habits.

"SHOULDING" ON OTHERS

Many people who "should" on themselves also "should" on other people. Of course, in addition to leading to anxiety, these

> Strategy #53: Stop "shoulding" on others.

thoughts can lead to anger and frustration. It can also interfere with relationships. Be mindful of when your clients use imperatives and judgments against others during therapy. It can be useful to point out that people have different values and different perspectives that will cause them to behave in a certain way. The futility of making judgments may be noted. Socratic questioning can help them to reduce these judgments.

For example, if Ellie were upset because she doesn't think that Rick does his fair share and says "Rick needs to do more," you could approach Ellie with the following questions:

- What will happen if Rick doesn't do more?
- Do you have a plan to get him to do more?
- How much control do you have over Rick?
- Do you think that Rick has a different work ethic than you?
- What do you have to gain by thinking in this way?

- Are there advantages to accepting that Rick doesn't do more?
- What are your options if Rick doesn't do what you want him to do?

Depending upon what the situation is with Rick and Ellie, problem solving may be helpful. Perhaps thinking about "the want" and expressing that to Rick could be helpful.

In conclusion, imperatives, whether directed at others or at oneself, can cause a great deal of stress in people's lives. The most helpful strategy is to find "the want" to replace these imperatives.

THE SOCRATIC METHOD

The Socratic method is a way to help individuals to change perspective by asking them questions rather than *telling* them what you think. Socratic questioning may be intended to evoke a specific positive conclusion. However, some cognitive therapists contend that it is better not to have a preconceived answer in mind, but rather to encourage the client to explore different possibilities. Regardless, the intention is for the client to learn and hopefully arrive at more positive conclusions. Below is an example of some Socratic questioning.

1. How do you feel when you are worried?
2. Are you glad that you worried about your test yesterday?
3. How is worrying about tomorrow useful?
4. Would it be more useful to problem solve?
5. Do you think things would have turned out worse if you had not worried?
6. How often do things turn out better than you had feared?
7. Looking back on the situation, is there anything you would do differently if you had it to do over?
8. How much does that event matter now?

SUPERSTITIOUS WORRY

When two things correlate, some people may believe that one causes the other, and behave as if it is true. When there is no cause-and-effect relationship between these two things, but one behaves as if there were, it is called superstitious behavior. Some people with GAD are afraid to not worry due to superstitious beliefs. They believe that somehow worrying magically protects them from having really awful things happen to them. They may be afraid that they will be caught off guard. This is not to be confused with due diligence, in which people appropriately believe in planning and problem solving to prevent bad things from happening. Rather, the worry is completely useless, but the anxious client feels as if the worry is protecting them or somehow causing events to turn out well. Sometimes they recognize at an intellectual level that the worries are superstitious and thereby useless; sometimes insight is poor.

Helping your clients to change their superstitious behaviors with a Socratic approach can help. For instance, ask them to explain how worrying would actually change events?

> Strategy #54: Identify superstitious worry and use a Socratic approach.

If their answer defends this way of thinking, ask if they have any evidence this is true. You may also ask if they have any evidence against it. Some people say something like this: "I've worried all my life, and nothing tragic has happened." In this case, point out that these two things are merely correlates and that there is no indication of a cause-and-effect relationship.

In some cases, labeling these worries as superstitious, can be helpful. It is also useful to explain that while this false sense of control provides a type of comfort on one hand, on the other the worry has caused them to be more out of control. After all, they are seeing a therapist because their worry has caused them significant discomfort. The very worry they believe is giving them more control is actually causing them to be out of control in the form of insomnia, feeling keyed-up, muscle tension, irritability, as well as in a variety of other ways. Encourage your client to do problem solving and planning in lieu of worrying to help control their lives in a positive and productive way.

Finally, behavioral experiments can be helpful. Ask your client if they would be willing to alternate days or weeks of using strategies to manage worry, including problem solving (see Chapter 4), and purposefully worrying. If so, ask them to keep a record of how the days unfold with respect to both positive things and unwanted things happening.

IDENTIFY WORRY AS LIVING IN FICTION

When people worry about the future, their thoughts create a type of artificial reality. This reality is fictional, but they feel as if it were true. Remember Emily earlier in the book? She was fearful that her husband had been in a terrible car accident. That car accident was a fictional account of what might happen, yet she was feeling as if her husband had really been in a car wreck and was badly injured. She had no evidence that he was in

Strategy #55: Worry is Fiction

a car wreck as he had frequently been late and been fine. Similarly, David, in the same chapter, was worried in the evening that the following day would be a disaster. He too was experiencing an alternate reality, feeling as if the day would unfold into a series of unfortunate events. In David's case too, the threat of a self-fulfilling prophecy was present such that his anxiety could keep him awake causing him to be very tired the next day.

Simply labeling catastrophic thinking in this manner as "living in fiction," "an artificial reality," or "an alternate reality" can be helpful. So, for instance, if you were seeing David in your office the day before his presentation you could say, "David, you are living an artificial reality. Yet you're feeling as if this fiction is reality and it's causing you undue distress. What are the skills you have learned that could help you to feel better about tomorrow and possibly create a better reality?" Additional Socratic questions, like: "How often do things turn out better than you had feared?" can be useful.

HUMOR

When possible, adding humor can be helpful, particularly when your client can use this humor to deal with their anxiety in the future.

Strategy #56: Embellish worry in a humorous way.

One way to do that is by embellishing their fears. This is particularly helpful when clients can realize that their feared outcomes are ridiculous. In the movie *Amélie,* the writers Jean-Pierre Jeunet and Guillaume Laurant (Miramax, 2001) do a great job of embellishing a worry of Amélie's. Amélie had left a photo for Nino with a note that she had torn into pieces like a puzzle. She expected he'd assemble it and receive the message to meet her at the cafe in which she works at 4pm. Once the clock hits 10 after 4 the film shows a hilarious series of events of the images that are going on in her mind with the following narration:

> *Nino is late. Amélie can see only two explanations. One, he didn't get the photo. Two, before he could assemble it a gang of bank robbers took him hostage. The cops gave chase. The robbers got away, but they caused a crash. When he came to, he'd lost his memory. An ex-con picked him up, mistook him for a fugitive and shipped him to Istanbul. There he met some Afghan raiders who took him to steal some Russian warheads. But their truck hit a mine in Tajikistan. He*

survived, took to the hills, and became a Mujahedin. Amélie refuses to get upset for a guy who'll eat borscht all his life in a hat like a tea cozy.

Clients often see the parallel between Amélie's thinking and their own. Helping clients to create a similar "over the top" humorous script with their own worries can be helpful. While the preceding took a worry to an extreme to add humor, the following is a script that I developed for individuals who have panic attacks and fear fainting in public, a common fear amongst individuals who have panic disorder:

What if you faint at the grocery store, fall onto the oranges and several oranges tumble to the floor with you and someone calls 911? Everyone in the store gathers around to look at you. You have orange juice in your hair and on your face. When the paramedics arrive they cannot contain their laughter. A kid takes a video of it and posts it online. You watch it in horror as you realize three people you know were there watching the whole thing. The whole town talks about it and nobody wants to be seen with you or associate with you and you wind up all alone.

Whether it be worry or panic attacks, going to an extreme can provide humor and be therapeutic. Be sure that you have developed a rapport and that your client recognizes that their fears are extreme before engaging in humor around these situations. You certainly don't want to give your client the impression that you are laughing at them.

Once I was doing exposure therapy with a client who had panic attacks and feared that walking bridges would collapse. We were standing near a seam of the walking bridge, and I said something like this: "Okay, if this bridge were to collapse, it would likely be right here at the weakest spot, the seam." He agreed. I began jumping near the seam and asked that he jump too. Exposure therapy can be very hard work, and adding humor can make it a little more tolerable. However, avoid using humor to the point of distracting them from the fear as this can be negatively reinforcing. To learn about negative reinforcement and why you wouldn't want to use distraction during exposure therapy, proceed to Chapter 8.

WORRY PREDICTION LOG

As mentioned in the first chapter, Borkovec et al., (1999) found that when individuals with GAD used worry prediction logs, outcomes usually turned out better than feared. And when worries turned out as bad as they had feared, they were handled better than expected. While individuals

<table>
<tr><td>Strategy #57: Worry Prediction Log</td></tr>
</table>

may have insight into this fact, they still have difficulty internalizing emotionally what they know intellectually. Monitoring can help clients to process this more effectively (See below). They repeatedly see that they almost always either experience a better outcome than they had feared or handle the worried-about-outcome better than they had feared. The result is that they internalize this fact better such that they worry less.

Worry	Reality – description	Rating	IF 3 or above How handled

Rating

1 = Much better than feared
2 = Better than feared
3 = About the same as feared
4 = Worse than feared
5 = Much worse than feared.

SECTION TWO

NEGATIVE REINFORCEMENT AND EXPOSURE THERAPIES

When clients avoid and escape their fears, both their anxiety and the behaviors that serve to temporarily reduce their anxiety are inadvertently strengthened, or at least maintained. This process is called negative reinforcement and usually causes a vicious cycle resulting in anxiety becoming progressively more severe. Identifying client behaviors that lead to negative reinforcement, reducing them, and eventually eliminating them, often plays a crucial role in the treatment of anxiety, particularly when treating panic, phobias, social anxiety disorder, and OCD.

Exposure therapy involves systematically approaching the feared stimuli, thereby preventing avoidance and the negative reinforcement of anxiety. *In vivo* and imaginal exposure are traditional methods of treating panic and the phobic situations that often trigger attacks. More recently exposure involves facing physiological symptoms of panic, repeating the feared thoughts, and using technology to face fears that often trigger a panic attack in the individual. Response prevention is used with all exposure therapy to prevent clients from escaping fears. In the next three chapters you will learn about the role of negative reinforcement in anxiety and how to use an array of exposure therapies with response prevention in the treatment of panic attacks and related anxiety.

CHAPTER EIGHT

The Power of Negative Reinforcement

Negative reinforcement occurs when a behavior is increased as a result of removing an aversive stimulus. Negative reinforcement is often confused with positive punishment. However, positive punishment is adding an aversive stimulus such that a behavior is decreased. An example of positive punishment is a teenager who has to do extra chores because he didn't clean up after himself after making a late night snack. As a result he doesn't leave a mess in the future. Some very common examples of negative reinforcement include:

1. Taking a shower removes a bad smell and feeling of being dirty (the feeling of being clean is positive reinforcement, too). The behavior of showering increases when feeling dirty and smelling bad.

2. Taking an aspirin decreases pain. The behavior of taking an aspirin when one has a headache increases.

3. Feeding a parking meter prevents getting a parking ticket. The behavior of feeding the meter increases.

4. Visiting one's mother decreases guilt. The frequency of visiting one's mother increases.

Negative reinforcement is a form of *operant conditioning*, also called *instrumental conditioning*. Operant conditioning is the learning that occurs when an individual's

> Strategy #58: Avoid negatively reinforcing clients' fears.

behavior is modified by its consequences. The behavior may change in frequency, strength, and form. Understanding negative reinforcement is usually more complete when contrasted with the other forms of operant conditioning which are defined by whether a stimulus is added or subtracted and whether those stimuli result in an increase or decrease in behavior. Note that emotional responses often change along with the behaviors. Below is a chart of operant conditioning with an example of each type:

	Apply Stimulus (+)	Remove a Stimulus (−)
Increases Behavior	*Positive Reinforcement*: Jonathan studies more after receiving a good grade on his test and praise from others.	*Negative Reinforcement*: Emma avoids driving to avoid feeling anxious when driving.
Decreases Behavior	*Positive Punishment*: Jenny drives the speed limit after getting a speeding ticket.	*Negative Punishment*: Ethan and Riley fight less while playing games after their Xbox is taken away for a day.

Any time a client behaves in such a way as to avoid, reduce, or escape anxiety, that behavior is likely to do two things: 1. increase those avoidance behaviors, and 2. increase the anxiety associated with facing the feared stimulus. This may appear to contradict what was presented earlier: coping strategies designed to reduce and avoid worrying. However, treatment designed to avoid worry is different for at least three reasons. First, worry is often used as an attempt to try to prevent frightening things from happening, such that decreasing worry may actually feel as if one is relinquishing control and increasing the risk that fearful events might occur. Second, because excessive worry involves a lack of parasympathetic tone rather than sympathetic nervous system activation, there is much less possibility of negative reinforcement occurring than their is in panic and in phobic situations. Third, given that the crux of worry treatment is to catch anxiety early and prevent it from spiraling, these coping strategies do not involve escaping any significant level of fear. Furthermore, it is conceivable that prior cognitive-behavioral treatments for worry were ineffective partly because clients waited until their anxiety was high before intervening, and did negatively reinforce anxiety. While this is unknown, there is plenty of empirical support indicating that coping strategies designed to reduce worry are effective in reducing anxiety when combined with early cue detection.

Unfortunately, in an attempt to comfort clients, many therapists inadvertently negatively reinforce their clients' anxiety. This is a natural response. Therapists want to comfort their clients, not make them feel worse. Yet in the long run, the temporary comfort that is provided only serves to maintain and even strengthen the discomfort.

By giving reassurance or encouraging any number of negatively-reinforcing behaviors, you may actually increase clients' fear and anxiety. For example, let's say that Ryan is having panic attacks and is fearful of having a heart attack. When he has this fear, he feels compelled to check his heart rate to make sure it is beating consistently. He also reassures himself that his doctor has run every test imaginable and that he is fine. While these behaviors temporarily reduce his anxiety, he quickly rebounds with the thought: "What if the doctor missed something?" and checks his heart rate again. This cycle may repeat for several minutes or even hours, "ping-ponging" back and forth between anxious thoughts and feelings on the one hand and reassuring thoughts and checking his heart on the other hand. Each time, he negatively reinforces both the anxiety and the urge to self-reassure and check his heart. His therapist may try to use what they think is cognitive therapy by reassuring him and encouraging him to check his heart rate:

> *Ryan, your heart is fine. All of the tests prove that your heart is strong. You need to stop worrying about your heart, because your doctors have reassured you that you have a clean bill of health. I'm sure your doctors didn't miss anything. And if checking your heart helps you to feel better maybe it would be helpful for you to check your pulse longer in the future and let your anxiety reduce more before you pull your finger off of your pulse. Use your breathing exercises to help calm you as well. Also, if you think it would make you feel better to get a second opinion from a doctor, go ahead and do that. I know it's only your anxiety, but if it will help to reduce your anxiety to repeat the tests with another physician, by all means do that.*

The therapist in this script is trying to reassure him and get him to see that there is nothing wrong with his heart. However, reassurance is not only ineffective with individuals who suffer from panic, it usually negatively reinforces it. Hearing the above might make Ryan feel better for a few minutes and as long as a few days. Nonetheless, in situations like this, the anxiety maintains or is even exacerbated in the long run. Seeing a physician for a repeat of the test or a second opinion is often helpful for a week or two, but also typically becomes negatively reinforcing as well.

It is also typical for one medical fear to switch to another. For instance, Ryan may decide that his heart is okay and stop worrying about his heart, only to develop the fear that he has a brain tumor. After getting a CT scan he may decide he doesn't have a brain tumor, but then begins to panic that he will have an aneurysm, and so forth.

If you, or your clients, are having problems grasping how this difficult concept of negative reinforcement works, *The Little Shop of Horrors* provides a great analogy. It is probably best known as a film (Geffen & Oz, 1987), although it was first a book and then a musical play. It's not necessary to be familiar with the story to understand its relevance to negative reinforcement. In *The Little Shop of Horrors, a* character by the name of Seymour purchases a small venus fly trap which he names "Audrey Jr." The plant starts off meekly and relatively infrequently asking Seymour to "feed me." After Seymour feeds the plant, it is quiet, and Seymour is relieved to have some peace. However, the plant grows and soon becomes hungry again, only to beg a little louder and a little more persistently. Each time Seymour feeds Audrey Jr. it temporarily quiets it, only to wind up making it grow larger, louder, and become more persistent in its begging to be fed. Eventually, the once small plant becomes so large and so out of control that it is insatiable and tries to eat people.

In this story, Seymour is negatively reinforced. His behavior of feeding Audrey Jr. is reinforced by a temporary break from the plant's begging such that he continually feeds it only to find the begging become worse. This is analogous to panic disorder as well as agoraphobia, OCD, and specific phobias. The plant is akin to panic disorder, feeding the plant is analogous to escape, avoidance, checking, and reassurance, and the begging is analogous to anxiety. In order to stop the begging, Seymour would need to starve the plant by refraining from feeding Audrey Jr. While this would certainly lead to more persistence on the part of Audrey Jr. in the short term, in the long run it would weaken the plant, causing the begging to cease eventually.

SUBSTANCES THAT NEGATIVELY REINFORCE ANXIETY

There are many ways that people commonly negatively reinforce their anxiety. The most common is probably the use of medication. Benzodiazepines such as alprazolam (Xanax), lorazepam (Ativan), and clonazepam (Klonipin) are often very effective at reducing anxiety once a panic attack has started, but will not usually prevent panic attacks. Furthermore, nothing is learned about managing panic. When the medication wears off, the individual's fear of having a panic attack often surges such that clients feel the need to take increasingly higher doses of the medication to reduce their fear of having a panic attack, as well as to reduce the anxiety once a panic attack has begun.

Even with a slow taper of benzodiazepines, without CBT, there is a 75% failure rate. Panic or fear of panic rebounds such that the patient, or client, returns to taking the medication (Otto et al., 1993). Furthermore, in a meta-analysis (Gould, Otto, & Pollack, 1993) exposure-based treatments with cognitive restructuring yielded an effect size of .88 vs. an effect size of only .56 when combining CBT with medication (Benzodiazepines alone yielded an effect size of only .40). This suggests that medication interferes with CBT treatment and at least some of that is likely due to negative reinforcement.

If your client is using benzodiazepines, never ask them to stop taking them unless they are using them infrequently or are on a very low p.r.n. dose. Rebound effects of these

> Strategy #59: Slowly taper benzodiazepines with the help of a physician.

medications are common. For more information regarding the taper of benzodiazepenes, see the end of Chapter 15.

Similarly, clients often self-medicate thereby negatively reinforcing their anxiety by using alcohol and recreational drugs. As with benzodiazepines, increasing amounts of the substances may be needed in order to get the same effect. Referral to a substance abuse specialist may be indicated.

Other Negatively-Reinforcing Behaviors

There are several other ways in which clients negatively reinforce anxiety. It is useful to assess for these habits early in therapy. In the next chapter, exposure therapy will be presented as an effective strategy in overcoming

> Strategy #60: Assess for behaviors that may be negatively reinforcing anxiety.

panic attacks. However, if your client is engaging in negatively-reinforcing behaviors, exposure therapy will not be as effective. Therefore, it is helpful to stop these behaviors first or be mindful of their role in maintaining anxiety. Some of these negatively-reinforcing behaviors are observable and some of them are not. It will be obvious if your client is checking their heart rate or seeking reassurance from you. However, many of the negatively reinforcing behaviors in which they might engage will not be observable. For instance, Xanax in their purse/pocket or compulsive praying are not apparent unless they tell you about it. The following questions are useful to ask a client before engaging in exposure therapy:

1. *What have you tried to do to reduce your anxiety?*

2. *Is there anything you feel like you have to do when you are anxious?*

3. *Do you find yourself ping-ponging or see-sawing in your mind?*

4. *What do you avoid doing because of your anxiety?*

5. *What makes you feel safer?*

In addition to these questions, use the rest of your assessment to specifically guide questions to assess for negative reinforcement. So, for instance, if your client shares that they go

> Strategy #61: Encourage clients to stop negatively reinforcing behaviors.

to church regularly ask if their prayer habits have changed, because compulsive prayer is not uncommon in panic, as well as in OCD. When used excessively to reduce anxiety, prayer is similar to reassurance. They are both verbal recitations that can be performed in one's mind or aloud with the intention of reducing anxiety. Prayer introduces a different challenge, because it's not ethical, nor desirable, to interfere with our clients' religious values. However, in my experience, it is relatively easy to help a client reduce, or omit, the negative reinforcement involved in excessive prayer, while still respecting their religious values.

When your religious client prays excessively, they almost always engage in other rituals to avoid or escape anxiety. It may be best to help them stop the other ones first. Once they understand the rationale of negative reinforcement, they are usually willing to make changes. My recommendation is to assess for what their prayer habits were like before they started having panic attacks and make an attempt to go back to those habits. So I might say, "I'd like for you to continue to pray before meals and when you go to bed just as you did before you started having panic attacks. However, I'd like for you to stop praying when you are having a panic attack and when beginning to feel one starting. I'd like for there to be no connection between prayer and panic except in the evening you may pray for the strength to get past panic and you may pray for thanks for having a good day." So far all of my religious clients have been fine with this, even a couple of pastors.

If the person is fearful of having a medical issue, it is likely that they will go on-line and check their symptoms. It is also likely that they will check their body in some way. This includes looking in the mirror, checking their pulse, checking their blood pressure, checking their blood sugar, and having someone else look at them and seeking reassurance that they look well.

Finally, people tend to avoid anything associated with panic attacks, particularly those that have been severe. For instance, someone may avoid the clothing they were wearing when they had the panic attack or take a different route to work to avoid the place they had the panic attack.

Agoraphobia is common among people who have panic attacks. To meet *DSM-5* criteria for agoraphobia (*DSM-5*; American Psychiatric Association, 2013) two or more of the following situations must cause "marked fear or anxiety."

They are:

1. Using public transportation (e.g., buses, planes, trains)
2. Being in open spaces (e.g., bridges, large marketplaces)
3. Being in enclosed spaces (e.g., small theaters, shops)
4. Standing in line or being in a crowd
5. Being outside of the home alone

While some people who suffer from panic attacks and agoraphobia may approach these situations with intense fear, typically the fear leads to escape or avoidance. "The agoraphobic situations are actively avoided, require the presence of a companion, or are endured with intense fear or anxiety." (*DSM-V*; American Psychiatric Association, 2013) The escape and avoidance both lead to relief, thereby negatively reinforcing anxiety and the fear of these agoraphobic situations.

The following is a list of common ways that individuals negatively reinforce their fear of having a panic attack:

1. Avoiding certain situations altogether
2. Avoiding specific situations based on history of panic
3. Escaping situations
4. Taking a Xanax before an anxiety-producing situation (or alcohol or other drug)
5. Taking a Xanax or flask of vodka along just in case
6. Taking a safe person along to a feared place or situation
7. Making a list and rushing through a store
8. Praying
9. Leaving the store prematurely
10. Reassuring oneself repeatedly that he or she will be okay
11. Checking – pulse, blood pressure, face, phone, etc.
12. Superstitious approach or avoidance – often numbers – can be anything associated with a panic attack

13. Keeping busy

14. Anything else that provides distraction or relief, including breathing exercises.

15. Avoiding exercise

Education, Cognitive Therapy, or Reassurance?

What we tell our clients in an attempt to make them feel better can be cognitive therapy, reassurance, or education. Both cognitive therapy and education are sometimes helpful. For instance, a common fear that people have dur-

> Strategy #62: Use education, but avoid reassurance. Know the difference.

ing a panic attack is that they will "go crazy." It can be helpful to educate these clients that panic attacks do not cause people to hallucinate or develop a thought disorder. However, this information, if not internalized by the client, can become a problem. If your client doesn't believe it the first time, be careful about repeating it. If it is used repetitively, what is intended to educate can become reassurance that will serve to maintain or strengthen the anxiety. To clarify:

- The first time education is utilized, it's education.
- When it's used to alleviate anxiety a second time, it's more likely to serve as reassurance and is likely negatively reinforcing.

Similarly, there is also a fine line between cognitive therapy and reassurance. Basically, if a positive statement, such as: "It's useless for me to worry about an unlikely event," works persistently for the client, it's cognitive therapy. If the positive statement is soon doubted, then reverts back to fear, and ping-ponging between the positive statement and the feared thought occurs, then it is reassurance.

CHAPTER NINE

Traditional Exposure Therapy

In the previous chapter you learned how negative reinforcement serves to maintain and exacerbate anxiety and avoidance behaviors. Stopping those avoidance behaviors is called response prevention. Successfully treating panic attacks involves utilizing both response prevention of avoidance and escape behaviors, as well as exposure to feared stimuli. That is, exposure to feared thoughts, images, situations, and places. In fact, exposure is often necessary to prevent response prevention from occurring. In short, exposure is simply facing one's fears, and response prevention is preventing escape or other behaviors intended to avoid or reduce the feeling of fear.

When introducing exposure therapy to clients, explain that the old adage, "The best way to overcome your fears is to face them," is true. Then ask if they believe this to be true. You will see a range of responses from uncertainty to an emphatic "yes." In either case, see if you can get the client to remember an example from their life in which they overcame a fear by facing it. If they can't come up with a memory, people will often connect with the image of driving on the highway the first time. The first time is usually very anxiety producing, but after 10 or 15 times it is much more comfortable. Next explain that there are at least four processes by which exposure is thought to work: habituation, extinction, desensitization, and a cognitive shift.

Habituation is a physiological process such that with continuous exposure to a stimulus, the body adapts to it over time. For instance, when faced with a feared stimulus, the heart can only race for so long before it slows. Extinction is a behavioral process that occurs when the fear is no longer negatively reinforced. For example, if a client stays in the grocery store instead of leaving it to attenuate anxiety, their heart rate will eventually slow (habituation). Because they didn't escape their fear, the fear as well as the desire to escape will not be negatively reinforced (extinction). As a result of both of these processes, desensitization to the grocery store occurs. The individual is faced with the stimulus but psychologically is no longer bothered by it. Finally, a cognitive shift occurs. The person learns that they can face this situation without feeling anxious and recognizes that it is not harmful.

Initially exposure therapy was confined to *in-vivo* and imaginal exposure. *In-vivo* is Latin for *within the living* and basically means live exposure. For example, if someone is fearful of driving, *in vivo* exposure involves getting the fearful client into a car and asking them to drive. Imaginal exposure, is just that – imagining being exposed to the feared situation such as closing one's eyes and imagining that he or she is driving a car.

In-vivo exposure can be performed gradually or suddenly. The former is referred to as graduated exposure, and the latter is referred to as flooding. Graduated exposure with someone who is morbidly fearful of water may consist of taking the client to a swimming pool and first having them stand several feet away from it. Then the individual is asked to rate their anxiety on a 0-10 scale, with "0" being no anxiety at all and a "10" being the most anxious they have ever felt. I typically ask that the client move to a spot in which his or her anxiety will be in the middle to upper middle range of a "5" or a "6" or a "7." While that rating might go up at first, eventually the anxiety will diminish. Once anxiety decreases to a "3" or "4," and the client is ready; they are asked to move closer to the pool until the anxiety reaches a moderate level or move to standing on the first step. Then the client would move one step at a time, each time waiting until the anxiety comes down before proceeding to the next step. In a typical 40 to 60 minute visit, the client may only get to the first step or two. Then he or she would be encouraged to face similar situations between sessions. With successive sessions the client will eventually get to the point of submerging their head in the water. Longer exposures appear to be more helpful. For instance, Stern and Marks (1973) found that a single two-hour exposure was more effective in treating agoraphobia than four separate 30-minute exposures throughout the afternoon.

Flooding, as an exposure technique, in the treatment of aquaphobia consists of having your client dive or jump into the deep end of a swimming pool, as long as they are capable of swimming. If not, it consists of jumping into 4 or 5 feet of water and submerging their head. The client is encouraged to stay in the water and submerge their head repeatedly. The advantages to graduated exposure are that it is a kinder, gentler approach, clients can move at their own pace, and they are much less likely to try to avoid or escape the feared stimuli. The advantage to flooding is that if the client remains brave, follows through with the exercise and doesn't escape, healing is faster. The risk is that they will avoid or escape, negatively reinforce their fear, and then feel defeated and more fearful than ever.

Imaginal exposure with a client suffering from aquaphobia involves visualizing a place that they eventually intend to face *in*

> Strategy #63: Imaginal Exposure

vivo and then either gradually approaching it or flooding it in imagination. As with *in vivo* graduated exposure, anxiety ratings are to be taken periodically throughout the exposure exercise. Some people respond very well to imaginal exposure such that the image of being in the situation can generate moderate to moderately high anxiety. However, some people state that imaginal exposure doesn't affect them at all, because they know that they aren't actually there. When imaginal exposure is effective it is the best first step to precede actual exposure. It's much more convenient than doing *in-vivo* exposure and can serve as an extra step in graduated exposure such that the graduated *in-vivo* exposure will likely move more quickly. A script for graduated imaginal exposure follows:

Therapist: *Closing your eyes and visualizing that you are in your swimming suit and walking outside several feet away from the pool. Visualizing the pool, its shape and color, noticing the blue water moving, people swimming, smelling the chlorine, hearing the sounds of the pool like water splashing and voices. Noticing everything you see, hear, feel, and smell at the pool. What is your anxiety level?*

Client: About a 3.

Therapist: *Moving step by step toward the pool, feeling your flip-flops on your feet and the ground beneath them. Visualize and feel yourself walking toward the steps of the pool and when you're about a yard away, stop. Are you there?*

Client: Yes.

Therapist: *What's your anxiety level?*

Client: About a 4.

Therapist: *Good! Being brave, I'd like for you to move up to the edge of the pool and choose to stay there or take off your flip flops and get on the first step if you are feeling brave enough.* (Pause) *Where are you?*

Client: I'm on the first step and I'm feeling pretty anxious.

Therapist: *It's good that you're being brave. What's your anxiety level?*

Client: Six

Therapist: *Okay, just hang out on this step. Feeling the cool water on your feet and lower legs. What are you thinking?*

Client: I'm thinking I don't want to get all the way in. I just keep thinking about how scary it is to submerge myself.

Therapist: *Instead of thinking about submerging yourself, just notice where you are right now and know that you can just stay there. What's your level?*

Client: It's a 6, but it spiked to a 7 or 8 for a few seconds.

Therapist: *Continuing to just watch others in the pool* (pause). *See the sun reflecting off of the water and feel the warmth of the sun* (you want to fill time here to keep their mind from wandering off of the scene and to give them time for their anxiety to come down). *Feel the water, see the water, feeling your fear of the water. What's your anxiety level.*

Client: It's coming down. It's between a four and a five.

Therapist: *Excellent. You've already made progress. Just continuing to hang out here.* (pause) *Smelling the chlorine, hearing the noise of kids playing in the pool.* (pause) *Letting the process of habituation occur naturally. Just waiting while you are wading.* (pause) *What's your level?*

Client: It's only about a 3.

Therapist: *Are you ready to walk down to the next step.*

Client: Sure!

Therapist: *Okay do it. Imagining that the water is almost up to your knees now. What is your level.*

Client: Well, it spiked up to about a six, but now it's only about a four and a half.

Therapist: *Great! It's good that you're being brave. Just hang in there.*

Imaginal exposure is particularly helpful when *in vivo* exposure to the feared event is not possible, because of harm. Some examples of this include fear of death, fear of passing out and wrecking one's car, or fear of jumping from a dangerously high place. These are all examples of fears that lead to panic attacks. Imaginal exposure is also great when facing the fear is cost or logistically prohibitive, such as flying or driving in the mountains when one lives in Kansas but wants to travel to the mountains.

Regardless of whether you choose to proceed with imaginal exposure, *in vivo* exposure, or a combination of the two, it's best to create a hierarchy of feared events with your clients. A hierarchy is a list of feared situations that are grouped according to how much anxiety they provoke. Ask your client to make a list of all of the situations they can think of that they are avoiding. Then ask them to assign an anxiety level of 0-10, estimating how high they think their anxiety will go when faced with that situation. When creating a hierarchy, keep in mind factors that might make it easier or more difficult to face the situation such as time of day, having a safety person along, or having a safety object with them. For example, the thought of going to the grocery store alone or at a busy time would likely make it more difficult than having a safe person with them and going at unpopular times. (Although, some people feel worse taking someone with them and, in rare cases, people feel better when more people are around.) Whether they have a Xanax in their purse, they have water, or their phone, for examples of safety items, may also affect their anxiety.

It's easier to follow through with exposures if you and your client are able to include as many situations as possible that are at each anxiety level. I will sometimes take a piece of paper and write 10 at the top, 9 half-way down and then using three more sheets of paper for the remaining numbers down to 3. A sample hierarchy may look like this:

10

- Go to the A&P® (grocery store where first panic attack occurred) without my phone after work alone (when first panic attack occurred).
- At night, drive somewhere I've never been that is more than 45 minutes from the house with my phone.
- Go to Target® and go all the way to the back of the store by myself on the weekend or after work.
- Drive more than 15 minutes away without my phone when going to a public place.

9

- Go to the A&P with my phone after work alone.
- Go to Target and go all the way to the back of the store by myself early in the morning.
- At night, drive somewhere I've never been that is more than 35 minutes from the house with my phone.

8

- Go to the A&P with someone on the weekend or after work.
- Go to the Kroger® grocery store without my phone after work alone.

- During the day drive somewhere I've never been that is more than 45 minutes from the house with my phone.
- Walk to the park and back by myself during the day without my phone.
- Walk to the park and do the loop with my phone by myself

7

- Walk to the park and back by myself with my phone.
- Go to Kroger with my phone after work or on the weekend.
- Go to Kroger without my phone in the morning.
- Go to Target with someone safe and go to the back of the store anytime.
- Walk around the block by myself without my phone.
- Drive somewhere I have been that is more than 30 minutes away with phone during the day.
- Go to Target alone after work or on the weekend and only get a few items near the front of the store.
- Pick up the kids from school without my phone.

6

- Go to Kroger with my phone in the morning.
- Walk to the park and do the loop with someone with or without dogs.
- Walk to the park and back with just the dogs with the phone.
- Drive without my phone to Michelle's, about 15 minutes away.
- Drive with my phone about 20 minutes away to a place that I have never been.

5

- Walk around the block with my phone.
- Go to the pharmacy alone no phone.
- Go to the Kroger with someone when it's crowded.
- Walk to the park and back with the dogs no phone.
- Drive to Bill's, 10-12 minutes away – no phone.
- Pick up the kids from school with my phone.

4

- Drive to Michelle's with my phone.
- Go to pharmacy with my phone.
- Walk to far corner by myself no phone.

- Go to Kroger without my phone in the morning.
- Walk to the park and back with the dogs with my phone.

3

- Drive to Bills' with phone.
- Walk to close corner with no phone.
- Walk to far corner with phone.

Some therapists like to start at the lower-level exposures first, while others believe it's best to be more aggressive, skip a hierarchy altogether, and do exposure to the most feared events. Depending upon the client, my strategy is to start with the middle to middle-upper level. I believe that starting with too difficult an exposure puts the client at risk for avoiding, escaping, or using distraction strategies. When these things happen, no gains are made, and there is a higher risk of the client having a panic attack, increasing the fears, associating you with anxiety, and even losing the client. I believe that most of the time, the client is already facing "2's" and "3's" such that there is little progress made when exposures are focused on these lower items. Therefore, I usually look to the hierarchy items that are a "4," to a "7" so the client is challenged and feels that they accomplished something significant while not being too tempted to avoid or escape.

Ask clients which of the items they look most forward to being able to overcome. For instance, this person may be most motivated to pick up their kids or get back to their walking habits. Therefore, she may actually be more motivated to walk to the park and back with the phone which is rated a "7" than to drive to Bill's which is rated a "6." Even though the former is more difficult, it may be the best choice if she feels more determined and braver to overcome it.

It can be helpful to do imaginal exposure of an event just before one plans to do it *in vivo*. For instance, I commonly show people with a fear of being in an elevator the elevator in my building so they have a fresh visual picture of it in their mind. Next we go back into the office and do imaginal exposure. If that goes well, and there is time, we will get in the elevator immediately afterwards.

When a client's anxiety gets too overwhelming to the point of their stopping or asking to stop, let them back off some, but try to keep them from escaping. For instance, if you and your client went into Target together and, while you were near the back of the store, they began to panic and wanted to flee, try to come up with a compromise. For example, walk to the front of the store and remain there until the anxiety comes down or leave the store, wait in the parking lot until anxiety recedes, and then go back to the front or middle of the store.

Many clients and therapists will ask when it is okay to end an exposure. It's best to allow the anxiety to come down significantly. Ask, "How relieved would you feel if we stopped right now?" If the answer isn't "not at all" or "just a little" or something similar, then it's probably best to continue with the exposure. Other than that, I suggest "the rule of 3s." On a 0-10 scale I like for the anxiety ratings to come down at least 3 levels and to be at or below a "3" before quitting. So, for instance, if a client started at a "7" and came down to a "4" it would meet the first criterion, but not the second. Try for both criteria, but if short on time settle for one.

If you are new to exposure therapy, you may choose to use the rule of moderation for your own sake and the clients' sake. In other words, if you are not comfortable doing exposure therapy but want to be able to do it, then it is probably best that you start with the easier items on the hierarchy first. Sometimes when clients are experiencing a great deal of anxiety it's not easy continuing to encourage them to face their fears. Because it is contraindicated to stop exposure therapy before a reduction in anxiety occurs, it is probably best that you start with easier items on the hierarchy and, as you get more comfortable, begin with progressively higher items.

CHAPTER TEN

New Directions in Exposure Therapy

In vivo exposure has been utilized to treat fears since the 1950s, and imaginal exposure soon followed. In more recent years interoceptive exposure (IE), flooding anxiety-producing thoughts and words, and utilizing the internet and media have become useful tools in treating anxiety disorders. While these methods have been in use for decades, informal polls from my seminars have indicated that over ninety percent of therapists taking my seminar had never heard of IE and less than one percent actually use it. Similarly, few therapists use flooding of their clients' feared thoughts or the internet for exposure therapy.

INTEROCEPTIVE EXPOSURE

IE is most commonly utilized to treat panic attacks. People who suffer from panic attacks are usually fearful of the physical symptoms

Strategy #64: Interoceptive Exposure

of anxiety that they experience. These fears are five-fold. Not all people experiencing a panic attack report all five. First, the discomfort of the symptoms themselves are so unpleasant that clients fear having to experience them again. Second, the fear is that the symptoms will cause a physiological event that will cause them harm. This is often fear of fainting, but might be fear of having a seizure, a stroke, or a heart attack. They may or may not fear that this event will cause them to have an accident. Third, fear that there is something wrong that the doctors have missed despite having had numerous tests. These fears may be of cancer or a rare disease, but is more often about having a heart attack or stroke. In any event, the fear is that a medical emergency directly resulting in death, permanent bodily damage, or permanent mental damage (e.g., loss of faculties following a stroke) is feared. Fourth, fear of embarrassment after others see them blush, faint, sweat, shake, or otherwise notice they are having a panic attack. Finally, fear of losing control, going crazy, and either fear of being locked up in a mental facility or doing something awful or embarrassing.

With panic attacks, the fear is not centered around a place, thing, or event. Even though situations often trigger panic attacks, it's not as much the fear of these situations as it is the physiological symptoms of the panic that will be experienced in reaction to these situations. Another way to put it is if the client could be guaranteed to not have a panic attack, their fear of crossing the bridge or going into the grocery store, for example, would be significantly less or even non-existent. The fear is of the physiological symptoms of anxiety. While there is a large number of feared symptoms, the most common physical symptoms in one study were as follows in order of incidence: palpitations (rapid heart rate), dizziness, difficulty breathing, shaking, sweating, hot or cold flushes, derealization/depersonalization, unreality, fainting (Barlow et al., 1985).

IE is a way of systematically exposing clients with panic attacks to their feared symptoms by utilizing exercises that produce these symptoms. The idea is to mimic the symptoms of the beginnings of panic attacks without causing an actual panic attack. The client becomes desensitized, or habituated, to the physical sensations of anxiety such that when the symptoms come out of the blue, the client is no longer fearful of them and the spiral does not ensue. The goal is not for the symptoms to go away, rather for clients to become more accepting and tolerant of these initial symptoms of panic, such that they feel mild discomfort rather than going into full- blown panic attacks. As a result of IE, the initial symptoms that typically trigger panic are usually reduced, and the symptoms that occur later in the panic spiral usually stop completely such that panic attacks stop.

For example, Georgia experiences panic and agoraphobia. Her first panic attack was in her local grocery store. She remembers feeling detached like things were not real, she felt shaky, her heart was pounding rapidly (tachycardia), she became fearful that she was going to go crazy, she found it difficult to breathe (dyspnea), and she became nauseous. She also became fearful someone she knew would see her panicking, creating an intense desire to escape. Therefore, she left her half-full grocery cart in the store and fled. Georgia immediately felt better when she got out of the store; her fears were negatively reinforced. As a result, she was terrified to go into that store again and her continued avoidance further negatively reinforced her fears of having a panic attack in the store. Georgia's fear was not about the store per se, rather her fear was that she was going to have another panic attack, specifically feeling detached/derealized, shaky, and having tachycardia, dyspnea, nausea, and fear of embarrassment.

When seeing someone like Georgia whose first panic attack was under fluorescent lights and in whom the feeling of being derealized is present, it is likely that the individual is sensitive to fluorescent lights. Exposure to fluorescent lights and other methods of bringing on the feeling of derealization, such as staring or looking at an optical illusion, is indicated. After repeatedly staring at something under fluorescent lights she will eventually become desensitized to the feelings. We expect that she will still feel derealized, but that those sensations will become much more tolerable. As a result, when these feelings arise outside of sessions, she will be much less likely to have a panic attack. She will be able to go back to the grocery store, experience derealization, and accept the feelings, thereby preventing the cascade of panic symptoms.

A cognitive component may also help in the healing process. This is particularly true when someone feels that there is something wrong physically. When they see that these exercises trigger very similar feelings to their panic, it sometimes registers that if they can bring on these symptoms and the anxiety subsides after repeated exposures, there isn't anything medically wrong. Also, there appears to be a control element such that the client feels as though they are now controlling the symptoms by bringing them on, rather than the symptoms' controlling them. In fact, sometimes clients will actually do the IE exercises when beginning to feel panicked as a way to control them, and it is usually helpful.

Below is a real example of a man who had panic attacks as a result of derealization. During this exposure, he stared at a textured design on a paper towel we hung near eye-level for one minute under fluorescent lights. Then we allowed him to recover by looking at natural light, and then we repeated the exercise, until the anxiety declined. Note that instead of being on a 10- point scale he was on a 0-8 scale.

Table: Interoceptive Exposure of Staring Under Fluorescent Lights
(using a 0-8 scale)

Symptoms Induced by the Exercise	Anxiety or Reactions to These Symptoms	Similarity to the Beginnings of Panic
6	6.5	8
6	6	-
6	6	-
6	4	8
6	4	-
7	4.5	-
6	3.5	-
5	2	-

The first symptoms induced by an interoceptive exposure exercise are those symptoms that anyone would expect to feel from engaging in the exercise. For instance, running up two flights of stairs will cause tachycardia, dyspnea, and for many, sweating. The reaction to these symptoms is anxiety or fear which generates additional physiological symptoms. For example, fluorescent lights cause many people to feel derealized, but being under them does not cause tachycardia, sweating, or any other panic symptoms directly. If these symptoms are experienced when exposed to fluorescent lights, it is anxiety in response to the feelings of being derealized.

When doing interoceptive exposure, the goal is not to induce a panic attack. Rather, the goal is to find an exercise that mimics the panic attacks, particularly their beginnings. It's best to find the beginning symptoms of the panic, because if the individual learns to accept those beginning symptoms, they will be much less likely to have a panic attack. Therefore, you want to match the exercises to the symptoms reported on their monitoring (See the following form) and get a rating of how similar the feelings generated by the IE mimic the beginnings of a panic attack. It is common for clients to be quite fearful of panic and the symptoms of panic without having had a panic attack for weeks or even months. In these cases, the form below is helpful to assess for panic symptoms that can help you decide which IE exercises to utilize.

PANIC ATTACK ASSESSMENT FORM:

When having a panic attack how often do you experience the following symptoms:

N = never
R = rarely
ST = sometimes
U = usually
A = always

_____heart rate increase	_____chest pain or discomfort
_____sweating	_____derealization or depersonalization
_____trembling or shaking	_____numbness or tingling sensations
_____difficulty breathing	_____chills or hot flushes
_____feeling of choking	_____fear of losing control or going crazy
_____nausea or abdominal distress	_____fear of dying
_____feeling dizzy, unsteady, or faint	_____(other)_____

Circle the symptom or symptoms that usually come first. Underline the worst symptom.

It may also be important to know what the worst symptom is. While clients may learn to accept the beginning symptoms and experience a cessation of panic attacks or a significant reduction in the frequency and/or intensity of their panic attacks, they may still fear having panic attacks if they haven't faced the most feared symptom(s). When this occurs, introduce an IE exercise that induces these symptoms.

Below is a list of IE exercises in alphabetical order that often bring on panic-like symptoms:

1. **Head Up**: Sit and put your head down between your knees for 30 sec and sit up rapidly or stand up. Or stand and touch toes for 30 sec and then come up rapidly.

2. **Heat**: Drink a hot drink under a blanket or drink a hot drink in a hot car in summer.

3. **Hold Breath**: Take in a deep breath and hold it as long as possible, up to a minute. (Optional – listen with a stethoscope during and after)

4. **Illusion:** Stare at an optical illusion.

5. **Mirror:** Look at yourself in the mirror for 1-2 minutes.

6. **Rapid Breathing**: Set a metronome at 120 beats per minute or higher. Breathe in on the first tic, out on the second, and so forth.

7. **Spin**: Stand up and spin around near a seat 1-10 times. Sit in a swivel chair and have someone push you in circles.

8. **Stairs/Exercise:** Run up a flight or two of stairs.

9. **Stare**: Stare at something small (dime-sized) 2-10 feet away for 1-2 minutes.

10. **Straw**: Breath through a small coffee straw 30 seconds to 2 minutes.

11. **Swallow**: Swallow three times fast.

12. **Tense**: Isometrically tense all possible muscles about 75-80% of maximum for 30 seconds to 1 minute.

13. **Tie**: Wrap a man's tie around your neck.

14. **Turn Head:** Turn head side to side – use a metronome to keep speed consistent.

15. **Fluorescent Lights**: Sit or stand under fluorescent lights. To intensify the effect, stare at something while under fluorescent lights or look up at them and then look straight ahead.

Use the following chart to determine which exercises to try:

Symptom	Interoceptive Exposure Exercise(s)*
Difficulty breathing	Rapid Breathing, Straw, Stairs/Exercise, Hold Breath
Palpitations, rapid heart rate	Stairs/exercise, Rapid Breathing, Heat, Hold Breath, (caffeine**)
Chest pain or discomfort	Hold Breath, Straw, Stairs, Rapid Breathing,
Sweating	Heat, Rapid Breathing, Tense, Stairs/exercise
Trembling, shaking, jitteriness	Tense, Straw (caffeine**)
Choking sensations	Swallow, Tie
Nausea or abdominal distress	Head up, Spin, Turn Head
Dizzy	Spin, Turn Head
Lightheaded	Head Up, Rapid Breathing, Hold Breath, Turn Head, Spin (sometimes derealization exercises)
Numbness, tingling	Rapid Breathing
Derealization	Illusion, Mirror, Stare, Fluorescent Lights
Hot flushes	Heat

*in order of likelihood to produce symptoms.
**caffeine is a substance that can be used to elicit symptoms, but is not an interoceptive "exercise" per se.

When implementing IE it is recommended that you utilize the above chart as a means to find an exercise that is very similar to the beginnings of a panic attack. For a first IE session it's best to have at least 40 minutes remaining before commencing IE. The reason is that you want to have enough time to allow desensitization to occur. Less time may be needed for additional sessions. It's best to do IE exercises in the session the first time, following "the rule of 3s" to guide the number of repetitions. Teach your client this rule and encourage them to do the same IE exercise for homework. When giving IE homework keep in mind that it might be more difficult for them to do it alone. You may also recommend that once the IE exercise causes little anxiety for them to challenge themselves by increasing the time, the intensity, or both.

Whether the individual is elderly with medical conditions or young with no medical diagnoses, it is important to get medical clearance before proceeding with these exercises. The exercises will never cause a medical problem. However, if your client has a medical condition, it is possible that IE will trigger a medical event (e.g., if a coronary artery is ninety percent blocked, an exercise might trigger a heart attack that would have happened later). This is very rare. If your client has seen a physician for the physiological complaints within the last year, it is probably not necessary to contact the physician. However, use your clinical judgment. Remember, even if it is clear that your client is having panic attacks, it doesn't rule out a co-occurring medical problem. Sometimes people have both. Even if choosing *not* to engage in IE it's generally a good idea for clients to see their physicians to rule out medical issues. This is, however, tricky because you want to avoid alarming your clients by suggesting that they see a physician before proceeding with IE. Below is a sample script of what I tell clients:

> *It's clear that you have panic attacks. Panic attacks do not cause heart attacks, aneurysms, or any medical emergency. Panic attacks do cause you to be more sensitive to normal physiological changes in your body that others may not notice. You may have even experienced these symptoms before you started having panic attacks, but they didn't bother you. However, just because you have panic attacks doesn't mean that you have a 100 percent guarantee that nothing is wrong with you physically. You are no more likely to have a serious medical condition than any other 32-year-old man. However, given that it's been well over a year since you've seen a physician, it wouldn't hurt for you to see your doctor just to be on the safe side.*

When giving this recommendation, try to use a matter-of-fact tone in your voice and avoid serious-looking expressions. People who have panic attacks, especially with hypochondriasis, can be very sensitive to any suggestion that they "need" to see a physician. For more on hypochondriasis see Chapter 14.

If you have fluorescent lights in your office, this can be a trigger for clients' panic symptoms. It's ideal to not have them in your office, but to have them in a storage room or somewhere nearby. This way clients are comfortable and feel safe in your office, but you can do an experiment to determine the degree to which fluorescent lights factor into their panic attacks as well as to use them for IE. I use our storage room which is purposefully lit by fluorescents for this purpose.

There are naturally occurring events or stimuli that don't meet criteria for agoraphobia or other phobias that lead to symptoms associated with panic. These include exercise, drinking coffee, having low blood sugar, dehydration, and being in hot places. Clients often avoid these situations, thereby exacerbating their fear of these situations and increasing anxiety when eventually facing them. Coffee and soda drinkers will avoid caffeine out of fear. Some people carry water around to avoid dehydration, others carry food to avoid having low blood sugar, and others avoid or escape situations that are hot.

Avoiding exercise is particularly problematic in two ways. First, avoiding uncomfortable sensations produced by exercising,
such as increased heart rate and sweating,

> Strategy #65: Exercise and coffee as in vivo interoceptive exposure.

negatively reinforces anxiety. Second, exercise stimulates the production of neurotransmitters that help to prevent and treat depression and anxiety. A lack of serotonin, in particular, can contribute to anxiety. For clients who had been exercising regularly before the onset of panic, a vicious cycle ensues. Their fear of having a panic attack leads to avoiding exercise. As a result, they negatively reinforce anxiety *and* they begin to feel more anxious as a result of having lower serotonin levels. The anxiety increases, causing a more intense fear of exercise. Therefore, the reverse is true. That is, exercise serves a dual benefit of facing the feared symptoms as well as providing a physiological benefit. Therefore, resuming exercise is a treatment priority in once avid exercisers who have been avoiding exercise out of fear of panic. In these cases, I discuss a gradual exposure approach to exercise in the first session, typically beginning with walking and adding more intensity as the fear is overcome.

Unlike exercise, caffeine does not have a benefit in decreasing anxiety and can raise the heart rate and induce jitteriness. Unless the client really misses coffee or other caffeinated beverages, I wait until they have improved before adding caffeine back into their lives. At that time, utilize coffee as an IE exercise of sorts. Caffeine takes about 20 minutes to take effect. So it's best to either ask your client to start drinking caffeine up to 20 minutes before they arrive, or bring it to the session and begin drinking it early in the session. You can have a session as usual, reviewing how they have been doing since the last visit, for example, or you could have them listen to their heart with a stethoscope. If their anxiety is relatively low, you could even add an IE exercise that they have already practiced. Remember we develop a caffeine tolerance that subsides after not using it. Therefore, it will take less caffeine to cause jitteriness and increase heart rate. Nonetheless, clients are typically more tolerant of caffeine than they fear.

Regarding low blood sugar and dehydration, in the beginning I think it is best to educate clients about the similarities between panic attack symptoms and the symptoms of both low blood sugar and dehydration. Because it is not really healthy to have low blood sugar or be dehydrated, encouraging people to purposefully bring on these states isn't typically recommended. Instead, at first educate them about the usefulness of preventing these states. Then use response prevention by asking them to stop carrying water or food with them if they have used either as a safety item.

A combination of IE, traditional exposure, and cognitive-behavioral coping strategies similar to those mentioned in this book (See Craske and Barlow, 1996) have been shown to be very successful in treating panic. Stuart, Treat, & Wade, (2000) found 89% of participants to be panic-free at 1 yr follow-up and Craske and Barlow (2006) reported up to 90% panic-free at one- to two-year follow up. Group therapy using a similar protocol was also found to be very effective with 83% of participants panic free at 6 month follow up (Telcher et al., 1993). IE with cognitive restructuring was also effective in the treatment of panic disorder, with 81% of individuals being panic-free at two-year follow up (Craske, Brown, & Barlow, 1991). In addition, this study found relaxation therapy to be significantly less effective.

VERBAL FLOODING

Another useful form of exposure and response prevention is flooding thoughts by saying them aloud (verbal exposure) and preventing

> Strategy #66: Verbal Flooding

reassurance or other forms of negative reinforcement (response prevention). Verbal flooding or verbal exposure is simply saying the feared thoughts aloud repetitively until anxiety subsides. This type of exposure is particularly useful when individuals endorse the panic items "fear of dying" or "fear of losing control or going crazy." Related fears that are commonly seen for which verbal flooding is useful are fear of embarrassment and fear of a medical emergency. The latter may be associated with hospital phobia, embarrassment, being alone and having no one to help, or fear of being an invalid. For parents, the fear of dying is often associated with leaving their children behind.

Before proceeding with verbal flooding, rule out overvalued ideation. This is when the client truly believes that their feared thought is likely to occur. *Most* clients recognize on some level that their fear is unfounded and will often tell you before you have to assess for it. For example, they will say something like "I know it's stupid, but I'm afraid I'm going to go nuts." If they don't offer such an assessment spontaneously here is an example of how you might proceed:

When you're having a panic attack you often fear that you're going to faint. When people have these fears it's common to have mixed thoughts and feelings. On the one hand, your fear that you're going to faint feels very real and you're terrified of fainting and being embarrassed in public. On the other hand, intellectually you know that you won't faint or you know you're no more likely to faint than anyone else. You might feel as though these fears are true while having a panic attack and then, after you've settled down, you recognize that it's unlikely and may even think it's silly.

Most clients will shake their head emphatically or say "yes." When this is the case verbal flooding is likely to be very helpful. If they say "no" and tell you that they really believe it is likely that they are going to faint, use IE, other forms of exposure, or utilize self-monitoring of panic attacks to guide early cue detection with coping strategies. If they agree that the feelings their fear generates and their intellect are incongruous, then verbal exposure is likely to work well.

To illustrate how to do verbal flooding, let's use the example of Rebecca who is fearful of fainting in public and being embarrassed. In this case, I would ask her to say something like this: "What if I faint in public and people look at me in a negative light and I feel embarrassed? What if the doctors are wrong and there is something wrong with me that will cause me to faint, and I faint in public and am embarrassed?"

Usually, anxiety will escalate from the initial thoughts. In Rebecca's case maybe after she says this the first time her anxiety will only be about a "5" but after three recitations she starts to have images of it and it climbs to a "7." Encourage your client to be brave. It's useful for you to remember that they are troubled by these thoughts repetitively throughout the day, and that while you are causing a temporary surge in anxiety, within minutes your client will almost certainly feel better. In my experience, a significant reduction in anxiety usually occurs within 30 minutes. In fact, it's not unusual for a rapid reduction of anxiety to occur within a minute or two. For some individuals simply saying it aloud instead of thinking it, makes it sound ridiculous and eases their minds rapidly. For others, it sounds silly when someone else, for example the therapist, says it aloud.

If anxiety is too high or not high enough, try varying two things: whether you say it or they say it and starting the feared statement with "I'm afraid" or "what if." Sometimes this subtle difference can make a significant difference in how anxious a client feels. Again, choose a middle of the road response first and edge up to the highest anxiety. So for instance let's say that the following are verbal exposure statements with the anxiety level next to them:

Rebecca: I'm afraid that I'm going to faint in public and be embarrassed. (5)

Rebecca: What if I faint in public and am embarrassed? (6)

Therapist: You're afraid you're going to faint in public and be embarrassed. (6)

Therapist: What if you faint in public and are embarrassed? (7)

In this case, one could skip straight to the hierarchy items with an anxiety rating of at least "6." However, given that anxiety often increases after saying these phrases a few times, it may be best to start with Rebecca stating that she is "afraid" that she'll "faint in public and be embarrassed."

It is good to alternate with the client when possible. This allows a wider variety of exposure to the feared thoughts as well as giving the individual a break from effort without having a break from the exposure. With Rebecca, once this anxiety begins to subside while she is verbally flooding even to a "4," it is best to move forward if there is time. If time is short, it would be best to allow her to continue. Otherwise, it's good for you to give her a break by saying "You're afraid . . . ." and then move up the hierarchy.

It is not unusual for anxiety to climb in the middle of a session after a reduction. This is usually due to the client's having new related thoughts or visualizing it. For example Rebecca, might think "what if I faint and someone calls 911 and the paramedics come? I'll really be embarrassed then and I'll have a huge bill." Or she might visualize people talking about her afterwards. Because new thoughts or images are likely to come up, be certain to assess for this particularly when anxiety has gone up or even when it has failed to come down. Assess simply by asking, "Have any new thoughts or images entered your mind?" or "What happened in your mind to increase your anxiety?" When this happens, include the new feared stimuli in the verbal exposure. You may also instruct your client to voice any new thoughts that occur during the course of the exposure before beginning exposure.

At some point in the exposure, ask them to observe how they feel while stating their fears and ask them to observe when they feel the most anxious. Then have them repeat only the most anxiety-producing parts. While this may sound torturous, it will actually help them to overcome the fear faster as they are likely feeling some level of relief when saying the easier parts. Looking at oneself in the mirror can add to the intensity of verbal flooding. Similar to flooding the fears aloud, one can think the words in their head or listen to a recording (see Using Technology below). This is particularly helpful when verbal flooding is indicated and it wouldn't be appropriate for the client to flood aloud. Likewise, repeatedly writing the feared thoughts until anxiety subsides is often helpful and processed a little differently than speaking or listening to the thoughts.

Expect that sometimes clients will report that new anxious thoughts arose that they hadn't had in the past. This may lead them to thinking negatively about the exposures. However, these thoughts almost certainly are in the back of their mind or they would think of them in the future. It is very common with these OCD-like panic-attack-related worries to behave in this manner; one thought subsides to make way for another fear to enter. Put a positive spin on this by pointing out that the initial fears have subsided so they have made progress and the new thoughts will likewise fade. See Chapter 14 for more information about verbal flooding with hypochondriasis.

Steven Hayes (2005) encourages repeating a single word associated with the fear as fast as one can for 45 seconds. It's best to encourage clients to think about the meaning of the word rather than distracting them. How-

> **Strategy #67: Rapidly repeat or sing an anxiety producing word for 45 seconds.**

ever, Dr. Hayes hypothesizes that part of the reason this practice is effective is that the word starts to sound nonsensical, thereby reducing its feared effect. He encourages the use of one syllable if possible and the least number of syllables if not. I have created hierarchies with these fear-related words. So, for instance, if you have a client suffering from emetophobia, fear of vomiting, ask him or her to state all of the words that he or she uses for the act of vomiting and how anxious each one makes them feel. For example: toss my cookies (6), puke (5), barf (5), hurl (7), throw-up (6). Use this hierarchy to proceed with repeating the word puke or barf and move up to throw-up and hurl systematically. Eliminate "toss my cookies" because it is too long. Other examples of commonly used words or phrases connected to panic fears include: heart attack, death, stroke, faint, bees, snakes, crash, lose it, crazy.

I have added singing to these exposures. Use the tune of a familiar song, but change the words to the one feared word. One of the best examples of this was with a woman who was fearful of panic while flying. She likes show tunes. We ended up singing "turbulence" and then "bumpy flight" to the tune of the song *My Favorite Things.* Not only did it help to desensitize her to the thought of turbulence, it helped her to have a sense of humor about it. She actually sang "bumpy flight" to the tune in her head during turbulence on a flight and it helped.

USING TECHNOLOGY

The internet is invaluable for treating panic disorder when panic is triggered by agoraphobia or other phobias. Standard searches yield mostly written materials, or at best a variety

> Strategy #68: Use videos or photos from the internet for exposure.

of media. Search engines allow you to specifically choose images or video (e.g., many provide the following search options: WEB, IMAGES, VIDEO, MAPS, NEWS) that you can use for exposures. Therefore, after putting in search terms consistent with the phobia, choose either images or video. For video, you can go directly to YouTube®. Watching videos can be overwhelming for some. Therefore, you may need to start by viewing photos, or even cartoons, when the anxiety caused by the phobic stimulus is too high to tolerate video. I will actually print the photos and ask them to carry the photo with them and eventually put it up in their office or in their home where they will see it frequently.

Some examples of fears for which I have used video exposures are driving, flying, hazing, heights, bridges, and insects. There really is not much of a limitation on feared stimuli you can find on the internet. When using video, keep your client's hierarchy in mind. So for instance, if you are treating someone who is afraid of having a panic attack on a plane, assess the scariest parts of the flight for that person. For many people it's turbulence. However, some people fear the take-off or the landing most. Others fear being stuck on the tarmac or being stuck in the air unable to land. Regardless, build a hierarchy. It's very easy to find videos of all of the aforementioned situations. I recommend taking a 30-second clip and watching it repeatedly until the anxiety is reduced. Once that is easier, find the hardest part of the entire video and watch a 10-30 second clip of that difficult part repeatedly until anxiety wanes. Begin by watching the videos in the office and then send a link to the video or videos to your client.

Videos can also be used as interoceptive exposure when the fear of derealization is present. There are videos of moving illusions that often generate derealization when the photos of illusions don't elicit sufficient derealization. Derealization is very common when driving. My hypothesis is that when people get anxious while driving, they stare in an effort to be in control. The staring actually elicits derealization. Therefore, find driving videos and ask the client to stare at the horizon while watching. When they begin driving, encourage them to avoid staring at first. Once their confidence is higher, ask them to purposefully stare; a way to do *in vivo* and interoceptive exposures at the same time.

Recording programs and apps are particularly useful for both recording relaxation for clients and recording verbal exposures. Macs come loaded with Garage Band®. It is relatively easy to record relaxation, observa-

> Strategy #69: Use recording programs and apps to create loops for verbal exposures.

tion and acceptance strategies, and verbal exposures. In addition, just drag the end of the recording to loop the recording. A loop repeats what you have already recorded. Record about a minute of the feared thoughts and loop them. Once you have finished the recording you can send it to iTunes® and convert it to an MP3. If you don't have a Mac®, try Audacity.com. This is a free program you can use on any computer. It is also capable of producing loops and you can convert the audio files to MP3s as well. The MP3 recordings are usually large files that can make sending them via e-mail difficult, if not impossible. Box® is a free program that allows you to download large files and easily send a link for clients to receive the MP3s. There are tutorials on apple.com and on YouTube.com to help you learn to use all of these programs.

There are also apps that do loops. For the iPhone, iRig is very easy to use and free. You can record a clip and one of the functions allows you to loop that audio. The Android has a free app called Voice Loop, but it gets bad reviews. For $1.99 you can get the very well-rated Voice Machine. Given that new apps are frequently available search "vocal loops" or "loops."

There are also free metronome apps. Metronome apps are useful for IE. They were designed for keeping the beat to music. Use them to keep the rapid breathing and turning ones head from side to side interoceptive exercises consistent.

Troubleshooting Exposure Therapies

Not getting anxious: Many people don't get anxious from seeing pictures, watching videos, or doing imaginal exposures. It's not unusual for interoceptive exercises to produce little or no anxiety. *In vivo* exposures reliably produce anxiety and verbal flooding usually generates anxiety. Therefore, move to these forms of exposure if the aforementioned stimuli do not generate significant anxiety.

When people don't get anxious during exposures it may be that the stimuli aren't applicable or are too easy, For instance, if an individual is worried about turbulence, a video of a smooth flight may not generate any anxiety. Some people don't respond to imaginal exposure because they know they aren't there. The same thing can happen with video.

It may be best to combine exposures. For instance, when doing IE, combine two or more exercises. One example is staring under fluorescent lights while breathing through a straw. You can also combine types of exposure. For example, combine IE with watching a feared video. An individual may not be responding to IE if you haven't found the right stimulus yet. Sometimes you will need to try numerous exercises before you hit on one that mimics the anxiety felt in the beginning of a panic attack. You may also create your own IE exercises. For example, I once used a strobe light from an app in a dark closet.

Sometimes when people don't get anxious it's because they are accepting the feelings. In this case, it may be prudent to shift your attention to observation and acceptance strategies (See Chapter 4).

Finally, some people see their therapists as "doctors" and believe that they are much safer in their presence. In this case, you can remind them that you are no better equipped to deal with a medical emergency than anyone else (unless of course you do have specialized training). If that doesn't work, then you can try leaving the office while they engage in interoceptive or video exposures. Other possibilities are having phone sessions, involving a supportive person, or doing the exposure alone. If you ask them to do exposures alone, be sure to provide detailed instructions.

Getting too anxious: Sometimes people will get so anxious that they want to escape exposure. While it is best to face moderately fearful situations to avoid this from happening in the first place, on rare occasions exposures will trigger panic attacks.

Do not allow your clients to completely escape the situation if possible. Instead, give them a break and then return. Research shows that as long as people go back into the situation after a short break, exposures are still effective (daSilva & Rachmann, 1984; Rachman, Craske, Tallman & Solyom, 1984). It is not necessary to return to the intensity of the exposure from which they escaped. For example, if you are helping someone overcome their fear of heights and they were at the edge of a railing, you might ask them to walk up to about two feet from the railing or if it was from four stories up, to go to the third story. If doing IE, reduce the time, the intensity, or both. For example, if you are using the straw breathing, perhaps allow two small straws instead of one, use a wider straw, or simply shorten the time.

Decision Tree for Treatment of Panic Attacks

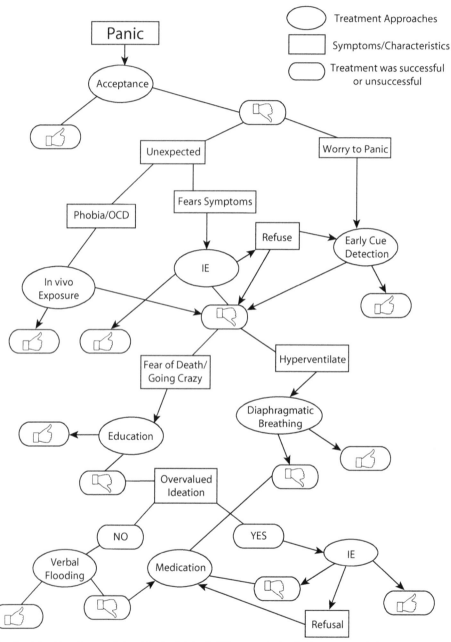

The Decision Tree is a useful guide. Individual differences in both therapist and client may indicate an alternative course of action.

COMMON CHARACTERISTICS OF CLIENTS WITH GAD AND PANIC AND HOW TO TREAT THEM

Individuals suffering from anxiety often present to therapy with a pattern of fears and habits that are not diagnosable yet contribute significantly to their anxiety. These clusters of beliefs, symptoms, and behaviors often require special attention in order for the individual to overcome GAD and panic attacks. The life patterns identified in this section are perfectionism, people-pleasing, procrastination, and hypochondriasis. You will learn therapeutic tools developed to specifically address each of these symptom profiles.

Social anxiety is particularly common in GAD. Individuals with social anxiety disorder often have panic attacks when faced with social situations and individuals with panic disorder are often fearful of the embarrassment if others notice their anxiety. However, social anxiety is not addressed in this section because social anxiety disorder is a diagnosable anxiety disorder with several books addressing it and it's treatment. One could argue that perfectionists have obsessive-compulsive personality disorder or that many procrastinators have ADHD. However, this is not always the case and because they are not anxiety disorders the literature doesn't focus on treatment for the anxiety associated with these conditions. Therefore, these issues and the treatment of the anxiety associated with them will be presented in this section.

CHAPTER ELEVEN

Perfectionism

Perfectionism is a common trait among individuals who worry excessively. People who suffer from this belief system are among the most difficult to treat. They do not benefit as much from CBT, interpersonal psychotherapy, and pharmacotherapy (Blatt, Quinlan, Pilkonis, & Shea, 1995). Even children who are perfectionistic do less well with CBT treatment (Mitchell, Newall, Broeren, & Hudson, 2013). The perfectionist's worries include: worry about making a mistake, worry about doing the best that they can do, being the best that they can be, and worry about what others think of them. Perfectionists often worry a great deal about work. Whether it is about pleasing the boss, becoming the boss, or fear of embarrassment about making an error, they set unrealistic standards for themselves in their careers. There is usually a lack of balance. Personal activities such as spending time with friends and family or pursuing one's passions and hobbies take a back seat to achievement and financial success.

YERKES-DODSON LAW AND THE PRESENT

One of the challenges in treating perfectionistic clients is that they are often afraid of letting go of their worries and their anxiety. They are

> Strategy #70: Introduce the Yerkes-Dodson Law.

afraid that if they reduce worry, they will lose their edge, and either make mistakes or not accomplish enough. Therefore, I suggest beginning by aligning with your client to help them become more efficient while being less anxious. To start, introduce the Yerkes-Dodson Law (1908). When presenting this concept, I like to begin by illustrating the myth that increased stress leads to greater productivity by saying something like: "Many people live their entire adult lives believing that the higher their stress and arousal levels, the more they will accomplish. I'm wondering if you believe that? Are you afraid that if you relax even a little, your productivity will suffer?" Then I will draw the following, leaving plenty of space to the right:

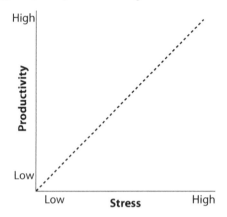

Next, I go on to say, "This is a myth because it is only true up to a point. It is a fact that if our arousal level is too low, we will lack the energy and motivation to be productive. However, when stress is too high, our productivity usually wanes. Think about the times when you are most productive. Are you most productive when you have high levels of stress? Actually, you probably don't feel stressed at all when you are in that zone of heightened productivity. Rather there is a moderate level of *arousal* in favor of stress. The Yerkes-Dodson Law has proven that a moderate level of arousal leads to the greatest productivity. Arousal can be fueled by positive factors such as motivation, excitement, challenge, or curiosity such that the relationship between productivity and arousal looks more like this." At this point I extend the line curving it a little higher and then down to complete the following graph:

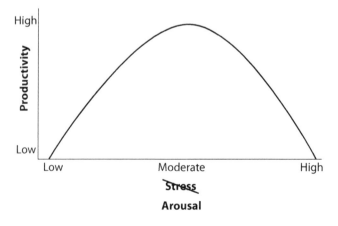

When working for short periods of time it is ideal to be right in the middle of the zone. However, most people work eight hours per day or more. Due to the fact that fatigue sets in over the course of the day, it may be best to actually lean a little to the left of moderate arousal. Otherwise, fatigue can lead to involuntarily lowering the arousal level and leading to slower work, decreased concentration, or mistakes. Therefore, I encourage clients to aim for the peak zone. The peak zone is a level of slightly lower arousal in order to conserve energy (See figure below). For most jobs, one can be in this peak zone cognitively and behaviorally, while physiologically being at a very low level. For instance, very little muscle tension and physiological arousal are needed for one to be productive at a computer, in a meeting, or speaking on the phone. Keeping physiological arousal at the lowest level to maintain optimal productivity will help clients to have more energy toward the end of the day to further maintain this productivity.

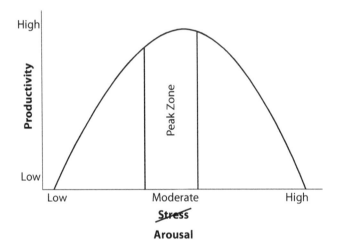

We are most productive when we are in the present. When in the present while working we are likely to be in the peak zone. Understanding this can help motivate clients to be in the moment. Approach this in a Socratic fashion by asking perfectionistic clients: "What are you doing when you're most relaxed?" Regardless of the answer I ask, "When you're fishing (or whatever activity they named) are you in the past, the present, or the future?" They will answer "in the present."

Next ask them to think about when they are working and they are at peak productivity. Ask them whether they are mostly in the past, present, or future. Usually they will answer "in the present." But sometimes they will say the future. Likewise, they may say they have to draw from past knowledge in order to do their jobs well. In these cases, offer that it is true that we want to reach into the future to plan and problem solve and occasionally look to the past to avoid previous mistakes. However, most people contend that when they are most productive they are primarily in the present. Avoid debating. Instead, ask your client if they would be willing to reassess during or after peak productivity.

TAKING BREAKS

It is very useful to take breaks. Many perfectionistic clients will state that they have no time to take a break. "I have way too much to do" is the frequent refrain. I retort with: "If you are feeling overwhelmed with too much to do, you cannot afford to avoid taking breaks." There is evidence that we can concentrate for only about 50 minutes. This is probably why a standard therapy hour is around 50 minutes. This is also why middle school and high school classes are typically about 50 minutes. The ten-minute break tends to rejuvenate and clear the mind, and the student can be refueled for another 50 minutes of study. Furthermore, it is a fact that regardless what the task is (mental or physical, complex or simple), workers engaged in an eight-hour day actually accomplish significantly less if they work those eight hours without a break than if they work seven hours with one hour of breaks (i.e., eight hours minus four 15-minute breaks). How is that possible?

I explain this by using a productivity quotient. The productivity quotient can be defined as a person's average percentage of productivity, with 100 percent being peak performance or the individual's highest productivity level. If someone works for 60 minutes at 100 percent of his or her peak performance, then that person's productivity quotient for the hour is 100 percent. If he or she works half an hour at 100 percent productivity and not at all for half an hour, that person's productivity quotient is 50 percent. If someone works 100 percent for thirty minutes and 50 percent for thirty minutes, their productivity quotient is 75 percent.

Below is an example of two workers who we will assume are equal in terms of their ability to be productive. While this is purely hypothetical, I believe the difference indicated is a modest one and is typically greater than indicated in this chart. After a break, most people feel revitalized and are so much more productive that they make up for their break within an hour.

Hour	Worker One Break-taking worker	Worker Two Worker not taking breaks
1	90%	90%
2	52.5% (70% for 45 min; 0% for 15 min break)	67.5% (70% for 45 min; 60% for 15 min)
3	75%	50%
4	52.5% (0% for 15 min break; 70% for 45 min)	37.5% (45% for 15 min; 35% for 45 min)
lunch	break	break
5	85%	85%
6	52.5% (70% for 45 min; 0% for 15 min break)	67.5% (70% for 45 min; 60% for 15 min)
7	70%	50%
8	45% (0% for 15 min break; 60% for 45 min)	32.5% (40% for 15 min; 30% for 45 min)
Average	66%	60%

Often clients continue to be reluctant to take breaks despite the rationale for taking them. In this case, I ask clients if they would be willing to do a behavioral experiment and take one 15-minute break at the point in the day in which they feel their productivity is low. Or, if they have a job in which they are allowed only to take scheduled breaks, to choose a time that is likely to be most beneficial.

One of my clients was very reluctant to take a break, but agreed to do an experiment on each work day between our appointments. When she came back to report on her progress, it was so successful that she didn't feel she needed to come back even after following up several months later.

She reported that she had taken a 15-20-minute mid-afternoon break and found multiple advantages to it. We referred to her success as a "win-win-win-win-win" as follows:

Win 1: She enjoyed the break.

Win 2: She felt much more productive when she returned.

Win 3: She consistently left the office earlier than in the past, because she got so much more accomplished after the break.

Win 4: She enjoyed the evening more, because she was less tired and more relaxed.

Win 5: She stopped dreading going into work. Therefore, she was likely
more productive at the beginning of the next day.

She learned that she did not have time to *not* take a break.

If one break is helpful, ask them to do another experiment and take
two breaks. Alternatively, ask them to be willing to take additional breaks as
needed when productivity and energy are waning.

When taking a break it is imperative that
people leave their cube, office, or other place
of work. Sitting at one's desk searching the in-

> Strategy #71: Encourage
> strategic breaks.

ternet, playing a game, or talking on the phone is not going to be very helpful
for most. It is okay to engage in these activities away from one's place of work,
however it is best to take a walk, read for pleasure, or do something else that
is more relaxing.

NEGATIVE AND POSITIVE REINFORCEMENT IN PERFECTIONISM

Many perfectionistic people unwittingly strengthen and maintain perfectionistic behaviors and the anxiety associated with them by negatively reinforcing
them. They feel anxiety when they have unanswered phone calls or e-mails,
for example, and when they finish responding to them they feel a sense of
relief. Or a client finally feels relaxed after trying on four outfits and spending
30 minutes on her hair and make-up. This becomes a habit and causes increasing amounts of anxiety when work remains unfinished, thereby making it more
difficult to leave these tasks undone in the future. This makes it difficult for
them to relax when tasks aren't finished or things don't feel or look "just right."

Similarly, there are people who work
well into the evening and on weekends. The
mindset is that he or she will do something
fun "after the work is finished." While this
works great for some people, for others the
work is always the priority and that break very

> Strategy #72: Stop
> negative reinforcement
> by making leisure a
> priority, leaving the
> in-box half full, etc.

seldom comes. As a result their lives are continually out of balance.

In this case encourage clients to schedule times where leisure is the priority. This can be time to themselves or time spent with friends or relatives.
During this time no matter what happens with work, it is their time. In the
beginning, clients may find it difficult to relax because they are in the habit of
putting work first. If they have work that is unfinished, they are accustomed
to finishing it or working on it until they are exhausted or done. When clients

are motivated to make changes they stop negatively reinforcing their anxiety by *not* working. With time, a combination of avoiding negative reinforcement and using cognitive and relaxation strategies, clients begin to enjoy free time and are positively reinforced, thereby strengthening the new habit.

Consistent with their desire to finish their work, perfectionistic clients often feel a strong desire to keep their "in-box" from being too full and get pleasure in emptying it or keeping it low. In addition to the negative reinforcement, another problem with this habit is that they create more room in the in-box to place more in it. It is harder to turn down additional projects because the client feels less overwhelmed. It is harder to defend why he or she can't take on an additional project particularly if it is from a superior. I believe too that many of these individuals have superiors and colleagues that take advantage of their high work ethic. In some cases, the work environment demands excessive work and hours. I have encouraged clients to resign from jobs that are just not worth the demands that are being placed on them. When they do, they usually feel much better and don't regret the changes.

While negative reinforcement is often a big factor in maintaining and strengthening perfectionistic habits, positive reinforcement usually plays a large role in maintaining them as

> **Strategy #73: Address advantages and fears of being less perfectionistic.**

well. This positive reinforcement can range from praise about their appearance, to feeling respected, to promotions and large salaries and bonuses. This can be very challenging as people enjoy the respect their titles bring them and love their fancy sports cars and big homes. Even for those who don't make a great deal of money, praise can be reinforcement enough to maintain bad habits. Gaining insight into the extent to which the costs of their perfectionism outweigh the advantages is a good first step. Therefore, making a list of the costs and benefits can be helpful. For instance, the benefits may be respect, financial security, nice car, nice house, and able to afford to send kids to college. Examples of the costs include: rarely get to enjoy the nice house, spend very little time with family, no time for hobbies, fatigue, headaches, weight gain, insomnia, dysthymia, and anxiety.

BALANCE AND "SUCCESS"

The hypothetical death-bed question can be helpful to encourage clients to create more balance in their lives. The question is: "On your deathbed, are you more likely to regret that you didn't accomplish more and make more money, or are you more likely to regret that you didn't spend more time with friends, families, and your passions?"

A similar strategy is to change the defi-
nition of success. We tend to think of success
in the form of accomplishments and money,

> **Strategy #74: Use the death bed question.**

particularly in Western society. Ask anyone in America who is more successful, a lawyer who makes $600,000/year or a librarian who makes $60,000? Of
course the lawyer is more successful in the traditional sense. But, what if we
were to define success more in terms of fulfillment and balance? If the lawyer
is stressed, unhappy, irritable, works 70-80 hours per week, and has no time
to pursue his passions, while the librarian has a balanced life, with minimal
stress; who is more successful? Who would you rather be?

Pam Houston put this concept very well in her memoir. Here is an
excerpt from her chapter titled "Redefining Success,"

> *... My first notion of success, came from my parents and involved
> country clubs, clothing, and cars. As I became an adult I replaced that
> list with a list of my own, no less arbitrary: a Ph.D., a book of short
> stories, a place on a best-seller list, a film. But now I am coming to
> the understanding that success has less to do with the accumulation of
> things and more to do with an accumulation of moments, and that
> creating a successful life might be as simple as determining which
> moments are the most valuable, and seeing how many of those I can
> string together in a line.*

Ask your client to close their eyes and
imagine what their life would be like if they
were 20 percent less perfectionistic. What

> **Strategy #75: Redefine Success**

would they have to gain? What would they be afraid of losing? In my experience it is usually possible to devise a plan in which perfectionistic clients
can maintain many of the advantages of their past hard work, while easing
internal and external demands. This can be accomplished by helping your
client to prioritize tasks. Help them to delegate or reject portions of their
jobs that are not worth the trouble. This often requires acceptance that
others to whom they delegate won't do the job as well. The goal is to learn
to work smarter, not harder, such that the benefits of changes outweigh
the losses.

The following paradox can be helpful for individuals struggling with
perfectionism: *Your perfectionism is making you less perfect.* Discuss the reality
of what brought them to therapy. Maybe they aren't sleeping? Maybe they
snap at their children? Maybe they have headaches or stomach aches from the

stress? Point out the irony that in an effort to achieve more, they have caused their lives to be worse instead of better.

This chapter was aimed towards working with individuals who are perfectionistic about work, because it is what most perfectionists worry about. However, individuals sometimes worry about being perfectionistic in other areas of their lives such as being a perfect mother, looking perfect, and socially (e.g. being the perfect friend or never saying anything wrong). Addressing all of these aspects directly is beyond the scope of this book. However, most of the concepts above apply to other areas of perfectionism.

CHAPTER TWELVE

People-Pleasing

Many people consistently put others ahead of themselves. In fact, therapists are often people pleasers who put their clients' and others' needs ahead of their own. Other professions people pleasers often choose are teaching, nursing, social work, and being a stay-at-home mom. Clients who are self-sacrificers often feel overwhelmed because they not only worry about the responsibilities they have for work, errands, and home, they also worry about friends, family, colleagues, and sometimes even people they haven't met. It's not uncommon for these individuals to take more responsibility for other peoples' problems than those people take for themselves. In fact, people who make taking care of others a priority typically put themselves last. They take little time for themselves and take a good deal of time helping others. It is not unusual for these clients to cancel therapy appointments to do things for others who have far less important things to do than go to therapy. Finally, they may spend money on other people that they wouldn't spend on themselves, denying their own needs and desires.

While there are many people who spend too many of their own resources on others, the world would be a dismal place if we didn't help each other from time to time. Good people help other people. Therefore, the goal of treating the people pleaser is to help them to continue to help others when it is appropriate and when they "want to" rather than being driven by guilt, fear, and "shoulds." Sometimes this is confusing. There are situations in which self-sacrificing behaviors are driven by guilt and anxiety on the one hand and a desire to help on the other hand. Help your client to sort through these thoughts and emotions to decide when it is best to continue to lend help and when it is best to set limits. This is a major part of helping care-taking individuals to heal.

Clients are sometimes concerned that setting boundaries will cause them to lose

> Strategy #76: Help people pleasers to stop helping out of guilt and fear while continuing to help when they want.

friends. Instead, creating boundaries will allow them to lose one-sided relationships with people who are taking advantage of them. Encourage your clients that they will learn who their true friends are and will have more time to spend with good friends. Also, ask them to consider that their lives will be easier if they end or take a step back from one-sided relationships, because they can devote more time and energy to the people in their lives who truly care about them. Be mindful that selfish, entitled people tend to align themselves with people pleasers, and vice versa. Likewise, these two types of people often marry.

NEGATIVE AND POSITIVE REINFORCEMENT IN PEOPLE PLEASING

Negative reinforcement plays a significant role in maintaining these self-sacrificing habits. While anxiety is often present, it is primarily guilt that is negatively reinforced. Fear of feeling guilty and fear that the individual being denied will get angry or feel disappointed lead to self-sacrificing behaviors. In other words, if your client has a habit of letting others take advantage, they will likely feel guilty and fearful saying "no." To avoid feeling that discomfort, they say "yes." Each time they "give in" they maintain or even strengthen that behavior through negative reinforcement.

Positive reinforcement is also a factor. People pleasers often identify themselves by their self-sacrificing habits saying as if it is a badge of honor: "I'm a people pleaser." They feel good about themselves because they are needed and helpful. They get pleasure from people talking about how nice they are and being thanked for their help. While it is certainly healthy to feel good about helping others, it's not healthy when one identifies themselves by the trait. Sometimes the positive reinforcement and belief that they are a good person for being a helper, is a way to compensate for feelings of inferiority. Like many mental health issues this is a matter of the degree. To what extent is the person harmed by excessive self-sacrificing behaviors? Do the benefits outweigh the harm?

ASSERTION

Because these clients are not accustomed to setting boundaries and saying "no" they may benefit from learning assertiveness skills. Some clients have the skills, but feel anxious about exercising these skills. Therefore, encouraging them to apply coping strategies when being assertive can be helpful (e.g., mindfulness, B^3s). However, facing the discomfort repeatedly (exposure therapy) will ultimately help the most. As they stop reinforcing the old habits, the new habits will become more comfortable.

A key to learning assertive behavior involves getting clients to take responsibility for their decision to say "no" by using "I-language." While at first glance "I-language" may sound selfish, it's received better than saying "you." For instance, if someone asked your client to

> Strategy #77: Teach clients assertive skills to say "no" to unrealistic requests as well as to ask for help.

borrow their car and they said "I'm not comfortable loaning my car to anyone." It's probably going to be received better than "You can't borrow my car." It might be useful to role-play situations that the client anticipates being an issue. It may also be useful for you to recommend a book on assertiveness. I recommend *The Assertive Option* (Jakubowski & Lange, 1978) because the concepts are solid and the presentation is excellent. However, some of the examples are outdated.

One concept that is not included in *The Assertive Option* is the *Columbo* technique which is based on the television series starring Peter Falk (*Columbo*, Universal Studios). Rather than being direct with suspects, Columbo acted confused and asked questions. This approach disarms the receiver making it very unlikely that they will get defensive or aggressive. Often it puts the receiver in a position that they want to help. The confused tone of voice is key in pulling off the *Columbo* technique. For example, a people-pleasing client had waited 30 minutes past the time she was scheduled for her relief worker to arrive several days in a row. She wasn't comfortable saying, "I was expecting you at 5." But she was okay with saying, "I'm confused. Are you scheduled to get here at 5 or 5:30?" It was successful; she was able to leave at 5pm after that.

Another facet to this care-taking habit includes difficulty asking for help. Asking for help is another part of being assertive and overcoming people pleasing. Ask your client about the times that they have *wanted* to help others and enjoyed doing it. Then point out that they are denying others the same privilege when they don't allow people to help them. Furthermore, people typically feel closer to one another when they help each other, rather than the relationship's being one-sided. Perhaps the best thing about accepting help from others is that people feel valued. However, it also lowers stress when others help; there is less responsibility.

Anger plays a role too. While clients with this affliction are usually accommodating and peaceful, they eventually get angry from repeatedly sacrificing their own needs for the needs of others – even when no one has asked them for help. Anger builds and they often overreact to the proverbial "straw that broke the camel's back." Then they feel shame and guilt. Identifying this pattern is another motivator to help encourage your client to learn to create boundaries and be more assertive.

Particularly if your client has insight and agrees that these habits are a problem, the guilt associated with creating boundaries usually doesn't last long. Each time they refuse or decide to avoid rescuing others the guilt lessens, and it becomes easier. Often a healthy form of negative reinforcement occurs as they are relieved of these responsibilities. Furthermore, positive reinforcement occurs when they have more time to engage in activities that they prefer and bond more with appreciative caring friends and relatives. Often self-esteem is raised as they start to feel valued without having to do things for others.

IDENTIFY AND HEAL THE ORIGINS OF PEOPLE-PLEASING

Often identifying how your client learned to be a people pleaser is helpful. Clients learn this behavior in many ways. Below is a list of reasons the person may have learned this habit.

1. One or more role models were people pleasers.
2. The client had a sibling or parent who had a serious disability or illness and was put in the role of being a caretaker.
3. Similarly, the child was put into the role of taking care of the parents. Perhaps the parents had poor boundaries and shared their problems with the child.
4. The parents praised the client too much for being helpful to the point of identifying themselves proudly as a caretaker. Perhaps they were punished if they weren't helpful.

While healing the emotional scars of childhood is beyond the scope of this book, I recommend experiential strategies such as reparenting (See Chapter 15), open-chair technique, free-writing or writing a letter to the parent or other responsible person. I regularly encourage clients to read the subjugation (the habit of subjugating one's own needs to the needs of others) chapter in *Reinventing Your Life* (Young & Klosko, 1994).

CHAPTER THIRTEEN

Procrastination

There are two types of procrastination, procrastination that works and procrastination that doesn't. For the former, tasks are accomplished with little or no repercussions. However, there is still often anxiety about the deadline. Guilt is learned after being repeatedly judged by "planners" that procrastination is wrong. For this group of "successful procrastinators" I recommend three things: 1) Embrace the positive aspects of procrastinating 2) planned procrastination (Abel, 2010), which reduces anxiety, and 3) discuss this plan with loved ones. Point out the advantages to procrastinating with an emphasis on their ability to complete tasks on time and do them well.

The second type of procrastinating is not successful. The individual suffers consequences such as bad grades, late fees, and problems at work. For this group I use small tasks, small amounts of time, or a combination of these strategies.

Some clients believe that they are a mix of the two types of procrastinators. That is, procrastination works in some areas of their lives and not others. Or they may find that procrastination works much of the time, but they have suffered significant consequences of waiting too long to get started on occasion. Finally, there may be some people who believe procrastination works well consistently, but want to appease their spouse or stop having to stay up really late the night before a deadline. In these cases, clients may want to adopt a combination of both strategies.

PLANNED PROCRASTINATION

Some people simply work better under pressure. Whether it's that they concentrate better, are more creative, avoid dawdling, or

> Strategy #78: Planned Procrastination

avoid going into unnecessary detail in which they would engage if they had more time, they achieve more in a shorter period. Many of these individuals have tried to be productive well in advance of the deadline and can't get motivated, can't focus, or are easily distracted by unnecessary details or other distractions (e.g., phone calls or e-mails). Individuals with ADHD are commonly successful in procrastinating. They concentrate better when the pressure is on.

Left untreated, successful procrastinators would continue to go through life procrastinating and generally succeeding. The problem is the anxiety and guilt that they often feel in the process. Despite the fact that they know their procrastination works, they worry about the unfinished product until they start on it. They often feel guilty that they haven't started on it yet. Even though they have a history of completing a project on time and well, they still may worry about finishing the project and doing it well.

With this group of clients, I encourage them to embrace their procrastination by pointing out that the benefits outweigh the problems. Most of these problems can be easily fixed by accepting procrastination. The main problems are those that come from a negative judgment of procrastination rather than anything inherently bad about it. These problems are: guilt about not getting started, anxiety, and nagging or other pressure from loved ones and colleagues who are uncomfortable with procrastination. The other cost of procrastination is often lost sleep – usually considered a small price to pay for the success that procrastination brings. Therefore, the first step in planned procrastination is to embrace it.

The second step to planned procrastination involves honesty. Based upon past behavior ask your client to identify when they will likely start to work on the project on which they are procrastinating. The third step is a corollary of the second: schedule the time by writing the date and time on the calendar. If they start to feel anxiety or guilt about the project, postponing the worry (See Chapter 3) to the planned start time can be helpful.

The final step is the simplest and most familiar to your client. All they have to do is stop procrastinating and start working at the time they would have in the past. The benefit of planned procrastination is that less anxiety and guilt are experienced in the days prior to starting the project than when procrastinating without planning it.

While not a step per se, it is often very helpful to get loved ones on board. This may be parents of students who procrastinate or spouses who get frustrated that their husband or wife "waits until the last minute to do everything." Sometimes discussions with colleagues or supervisors may be useful as well. Clients can begin these discussions by acknowledging others' discomfort with procrastination. Next they can explain to the concerned parties their view that procrastination is neither right nor wrong, but a different way of getting things accomplished. Perhaps the most important part for clients to explain to others is that procrastination works well for them. They can elucidate by reminding the other person that the times they were worried about their procrastination, everything turned out well. It's not necessary, but may be helpful to explain that their concentration and productivity level is much greater under pressure such that they end up spending much less time to complete a project than if they were to start on it sooner. It can also be helpful to explain in some situations, that the worst thing about it is the grief that they get from others who are uncomfortable with it. Once this conversation takes place, I ask clients to let others take responsibility for their own discomfort. And, avoid feeling guilty or stressed by reminding themselves how well procrastination works for them.

Planned procrastination will work well with most projects undertaken by "successful procrastinators." However, for very large projects like a thesis, dissertation, or grant proposal, it may be necessary to break it down into parts and set deadlines for them. Finding someone to be accountable to for each piece will be helpful in this case.

Planned Procrastination Steps

1. **Embrace Procrastination**. Recognize the positive aspects of procrastination and stop feeling guilty and anxious about it.
2. **Be Honest.** Based on past experience, when are you going to start?
3. **Schedule It.** Write that time in your calendar.
4. **Do It.** Maintain the old habit.
5. **Support (optional)**. Attempt to get support from planners.

COMMIT TO SMALL TASKS

Inch by inch, life is a cinch. Yard by yard, it is really hard. The preceding sentences highlight the rationale for the second section of this chapter about helping clients overcome procrastination. This chapter is aimed at the individual who is not successful at procrastinating. It can also be useful for those who are successful procrastinators, but are motivated to make compromises to appease others or avoid some of the other disadvantages of procrastinating (e.g. lost sleep).

This section is particularly helpful for clients who get overwhelmed easily or otherwise have difficulty getting motivated. Whether it is inertia

created by boring tasks or whether it is difficulty getting started on a long to-do list
or huge project, the best way to help clients

> **Strategy #79: Break projects into small tasks.**

overcome procrastination and get started is to find small doable tasks. Most
people agree that when we feel as though we have a few small things to do (say,
three) it's easy to get motivated to accomplish those things. But when we have
three big projects and thirty to forty little things on our minds, sometimes it's
difficult to do anything. People who procrastinate may get bogged down with
an overwhelming sense of responsibility that results in inertia.

The key to overcoming this is to help clients commit to smaller, easily-
accomplished pieces. Break down larger commitments. This can be done in
two general ways. The first is to divide big projects into subtasks and maybe
even tertiary tasks. The second way is to commit to a reasonable, specific
amount of time to work on that task each day or week.

Here's an example that many people can relate to: a messy house. Some
of your clients will complain that every room in their house is a mess and
that it is overwhelming to think of cleaning it. Often when they look around
and feel the gravity of cleaning the whole house, they lose motivation. It is so
overwhelming because it seems that any efforts would barely make a dent in
it. Therefore, it's easier to avoid it and continue to live in the mess.

In this case, it helps to start by picking one room that your client feels
would provide the greatest stress relief if it could be clean. Let's say it's the
kitchen. That still might feel like an overwhelming task, but not nearly as
daunting as cleaning the whole place. The next step is to pick one kitchen task
that would be easy to accomplish, preferably something that would take less
than 15 minutes, maybe even less than 10. For instance, you could ask them
to commit to throwing away all the trash in the kitchen. Or you may ask them
to commit to put everything on the countertops and tables away, or just one or
the other. Once they finish this task they will have a sense of accomplishment.
Albeit relatively small, it is likely to be a greater feeling of accomplishment than
had they haphazardly worked on the house without completing a specific goal.

Explain to your client that once he or she has completed this small goal
one of two things will happen. One is that after completing the small task your
client might feel unmotivated to do anything else. If this is the case, encourage
them to celebrate their small, but important, feat. Encourage them to make a
commitment to do the next task the next day, or if it's a weekend or day off,
they might even commit to another task later in the day.

The other thing that is likely to happen is that by accomplishing this
task your client will feel energized and might think, "It would be pretty easy

to clean off the countertops and they'd look so much better." In just a few minutes they have clean countertops. At this point they will likely feel proud of the accomplishment and again, they might be finished for a while or they might think, "I may as well load the dishes in the sink into the dishwasher" or "I may as well do the dishes." If they get this far, the only thing left would be the floor, and that would be an easy task for the next day. Or if they have time and energy, they might just find themselves finishing the job.

As stated previously, an alternative to choosing a small task or subdividing tasks is just to spend a certain amount of time on a project. It's amazing how much better a messy room can look after straightening and/or cleaning it for ten or fifteen minutes if no dawdling occurs. Depending on your client's motivation level and the type of task, you might decide together that they will commit to only ten minutes, or you might decide on an hour or two. Much like the subtasks, one might spend ten minutes cleaning the kitchen, for example, and then decide that they are on a roll and want to continue. At this point, they can set a goal for an additional ten minutes or just continue at will. I suggest setting a timer because it can help to focus attention on the tasks at hand. Be fast and focused, but not rushed. Encourage clients to disallow distractions from the phone, reading junk mail, or otherwise taking attention off the task. Alternatively, if interrupted by a very important call, for example, one can take note of the time one was interrupted and adjust accordingly.

The aforementioned strategies may not be as useful for a larger task like a grant proposal or a thesis. For these big projects it is useful to motivate clients by dividing them three to four times until they are smaller, doable tasks. When doing my dissertation I started by looking at big chunks – for instance: "write the introduction." This big chunk involved the following chunks:

1. Do a literature review.
2. Read the articles found in the review and take notes and highlight printed articles.
3. Draft the introduction.
4. Edit it.
5. Get feedback from my dissertation chair and finish the introduction.

I decided about when I'd like to finish the introduction and estimated how long each of the other major steps would take (e.g., writing the methods section) in order to decide when I would commit to completing these steps. I broke this first major goal of completing the introduction into the subtasks shown above. Next, I divided those subtasks into tertiary tasks that could be accomplished in about a week and wrote them in my planner (e.g., read, highlight, and take notes on six articles). Then, at the beginning of each week, I divided the weekly goal into six daily tasks (e.g., one article). I wrote each task on Monday through Saturday of my planner. This method allowed me an extra day if I had underestimated the amount of time it would take or if I had an unusually busy week. It also allowed a day to break from my dissertation if the tasks went well.

In addition, I did make a commitment to my dissertation chair to have each of the milestones accomplished. It helps to be accountable to others to stay on track, especially with large projects. Ask your clients to make commitments to you, friends, and relatives who support them in accomplishing their feats. Eventually have them rely on friends and relatives with whom they can check in on a regular basis regarding progress and goals. This works particularly well if they can find supports who are also trying to accomplish a goal or change a habit to lend mutual support.

I finished my dissertation before I left for my internship, something my chair had never seen done in more than six years of being a professor; others on my committee could only cite one or two out of hundreds who had accomplished this feat. I had been a procrastinator before graduate school.

THE BEST OF BOTH STRATEGIES

A third option is to combine the two strategies of planned procrastination and committing to small goals. This can be done by setting one small goal at a time and giving oneself a time limit in which to accomplish that goal. Ask your client to estimate how long a particular smaller task would typically take to accomplish in those final moments when procrastinating. For instance, say your client is a writer. Have them commit to writing a draft that is at least three pages in ninety minutes. Have them record the time that they plan to finish this task and avoid doing the things that they would avoid doing if they were down to the final deadline. Ask them to think about how much they are able to accomplish when working diligently after having procrastinated. The goal is to mimic the feeling and behaviors of working after having procrastinated by making a commitment to finish that goal on time.

This is particularly helpful with students. Suggest they time how long it takes them to read a page and highlight or take notes in a specific book. Next, using that data, they can choose a goal with a good stopping point (e.g., end of a section) that will take 25-50 minutes. Record the goal (e.g., read to p. 118

by 12:20). Shorter times are recommended for individuals with ADHD or those with particular concentration problems. Once the goal is completed encourage them to take a break before deciding on a new small goal.

Alternatively, the client can start with the amount of time they'd like to commit to a project and think about what a reasonable goal is for that time period. For instance, they have a free hour, so they decide to write two pages of a draft in that period of time. Whether choosing this option or the former one, introduce a reward before going on to another productive task, even if it is just relaxing for a few minutes.

ADDITIONAL STRATEGIES FOR GETTING IT DONE

Timing tasks can help to prevent dawdling. Thinking of a task as a game can add additional motivation. Ask your client to see how much they can accomplish in the delineated

> Strategy #80: Set a deadline to complete a small goal.

time. Add in that they get bonus points for keeping their body relatively relaxed while being focused and efficient. For instance, see how long it takes to unload the dishwasher with the least amount of tension without sacrificing efficiency. Alternatively, create a timed goal such as "I'm going to see if I can unload the dishwasher in less than eight minutes." These types of timed goals often have the added benefit of realizing that avoided tasks often take less than ten minutes, or at least less time than it feels.

Another strategy to combat procrastination is preparation. When avoiding a task, buy the supplies, set out the equipment, and set out any required clothing ahead of time. For instance, I had been avoiding installing my programmable thermostat. So, I went to the basement, got the drill, a hammer, and a screwdriver and took the new thermostat out of that annoying hard plastic packaging. It probably only took about three minutes to do these few things. However, it accomplished two things. One, it eliminated those steps so that my task was now simpler, and two, seeing the tools and the opened thermostat in plain view made it easier for me to remember and harder for me to continue to procrastinate so I could "just do it."

An additional example of this strategy lies in the case of the aforementioned kitchen. Let's say that your client had done everything except for the floor and had run out of the time or energy to do it. At that point, it would take them about a minute to get out the broom, dustpan, bucket, mop, and soap. The next day it will be a little easier to sweep and mop the floor and much harder to continue to procrastinate on that task.

This strategy works particularly well for exercise too. If your client is having a difficult time getting motivated to exercise, suggest that they gather their clothes, shoes, socks, and anything else they will need for exercise the night before. Have them set these things in their path or put them in a gym bag near the door. They can still procrastinate or avoid it, but if you combine this with asking them to set a small exercise goal it will be easier for them to get moving. To add a little boost to this strategy, use the B^{3}s from Chapter 6. For instance, "I'll be glad when I've finished it," or "Once I get started it will be fine."

CHAPTER FOURTEEN

Hypochondriasis

Individuals with hypochondriasis worry excessively about their health. Some have panic attacks in reaction to unexpected feared physical sensations. Similarly, individuals who have panic attacks often worry that there is something medically wrong with them. In fact, hypochondriasis may have only started after the onset of panic attacks. Sometimes these clients worry that they may die as a result of their panic attack symptoms. Some of them worry that their panic symptoms are not panic at all, but an indication that they have a serious illness. Others worry excessively about their health with no history of panic.

Sometimes people with hypochondriasis have OCD. While it is not particularly common for individuals with OCD to suffer from hypochondriasis, it is very common for people with hypochondriasis to engage in multiple compulsive behaviors. These behaviors are aimed at reducing the anxiety created by the fear of the symptoms; symptoms that are often created by anxiety or anxiety sensitivity. In most cases, clients suffering from this affliction negatively reinforce their anxiety by engaging in behaviors such as avoiding, escaping, checking or seeking reassurance. While these behaviors provide temporary relief, they usually result in exacerbating hypochondriasis over time. Eventually, normal fluctuations in their bodies may lead to fear of catastrophic outcomes.

While we think of hypochondriasis as a fear of having a disease, this is just the first layer. The deeper fear is what that disease will lead to eventually. This varies a great deal. While the most obvious fear is death, some have little fear of actually being gone. In fact, some have faith that they will go to heaven, a better place. Among the deeper fears that people with this affliction hold includes fear of suffering, fear of abandoning their children, and fear of getting sick and spreading the illness to others. An intolerance of uncertainty is not exactly a fear, but is common among people with anxiety disorders, particularly hypochondriasis. In other words, many fear the fact that life is uncertain, death is uncertain, and health is uncertain. This intolerance of uncertainty often leads clients to use worry as a false sense of control. Some people are better able to accept the uncertainty that life brings more than others who worry about what cannot be controlled. Certainly, we have some control over our health by living a healthy lifestyle, but even then health is ultimately unpredictable. Similarly, we can avoid engaging in dangerous activities. However, accidents, natural disasters, and tragedies at the hands of man, are not predictable.

In response to these fears, people often engage in behaviors to try to make themselves feel better. While these behaviors typically help in the short term, they usually strengthen fears in the long run. It can be helpful to tell clients "Almost everything you are doing to make yourself feel better is making you feel worse later." Support them by explaining that it's natural to want to reassure yourself and natural to (insert their specific behaviors; e.g., check your heart rate), but the same behaviors that feel good now are ultimately fueling the problem.

This is a list of the things that you may see people with hypochondriasis do to try to make themselves feel better:

1. Go to the doctor unnecessarily.
2. Avoid going to the doctor.
3. Go to the emergency room unnecessarily.
4. Seek reassurance from friends, relatives, and you.
5. Reassure themselves.
6. Search the internet for information about symptoms and diseases they are afraid that they have.
7. Check vitals – usually heart rate and blood pressure, but sometimes blood sugar, respiration, or blood oxygen.
8. Check other things physically (looking at eyes, complexion, tongue, feeling glands, etc.).
9. Make sure they have any number of things that provide comfort, like water, food, phone, medicine.

(See Chapter 8 on negative reinforcement for a greater understanding of how these behaviors contribute to the maintenance and exacerbation of anxiety and, in this case, fear of illness.)

For hypochondriasis, it is particularly important to keep clients from searching the internet. This is true even if the client has a significant medical diagnosis. Even the more reputable sites can have information that is limited, misleading, or can easily be misinterpreted. This "information" often causes the client to become very anxious or even have a panic attack. In this case it is best to encourage them to get information from a physician or other specialist.

Assess for ways that clients check their health by asking questions like: "What do you feel compelled to check when you're worried about your health?" Remember that checking their heart rate, blood pressure, blood sugar or other readings will usually make them feel better temporarily, but will reinforce their fear. Regardless of the nature of the checking behavior, the goal is to get them to stop completely unless they have been directed by their physician to check. Then learn exactly how often their physician would like for them to check.

Clients will often use the language "I have to" or "I need to" with regard to checking. For instance, when explaining their anxiety they might say "When I worry about my heart I have to check my pulse in my neck." Gently suggest that they be accurate and truthful about their *desire* to check. Point out that it is more accurate to say "I feel like I need to check" or "I have a strong urge to check." If they think or say that they "have to check" they will *feel* like they "have to check," which in reality they don't. In fact, the opposite is true. That is, if they want to heal from hypochondriasis and panic attacks, they need to resist these urges to check. Continue to explain how their checking negatively reinforces that behavior. Also, sympathize that while you completely understand their desire to check, because it feels better in the short run, it is maintaining and even exacerbating their condition. Point out that if checking were very effective, they wouldn't be seeing you. Most clients understand this and agree to try to stop. Those who are successful notice that both the urges and the anxiety lessen with time if they are brave and stop checking. Clients are usually pleasantly surprised by how quickly they improve after resisting these urges.

People with hypochondriasis almost always attempt to seek reassurance. Self-checking is a form of attempting to get reassurance, and sometimes searching the internet involves reassurance seeking. More direct forms of reassurance include seeking reassurance from you (their therapist), their physicians, emergency room physicians, friends, colleagues, and relatives. *Self-reassurance* is very common. When clients reassure themselves it usually ends up in "ping-ponging" between a negative thought about a medical tragedy and a self-reassuring thought used as an attempt to neutralize anxiety. For example, it might be "what if the doctors were wrong, it's really unlikely that they both missed something, but what if they did, there's no way they did, but it's possible I do have brain cancer, that spot in my head hurts so bad,

I'm sure it's just a headache and nothing serious, but what if it is serious?" In some cases these habits are severe enough to be diagnosed as OCD. The fear of the medical tragedy and the resulting outcome comprise the obsessions, while self-reassurance, seeking reassurance from others, checking, and other avoidance behaviors comprise the compulsions.

While it's natural to want to reassure your client, your goal is to get them to stop seeking reassurance. As a therapist, you want to ease clients' pain, so you will also be inclined to want to reassure them that they will be fine. In proceeding, be mindful of the difference between reassurance, cognitive therapy, and education discussed in Chapter 8. Proceed with caution. If your attempts to educate and provide a more positive perspective about their health are effective, then they are education and cognitive therapy, respectively. However, if your client uses this information to "ping-pong" between positive and negative thoughts or further seek reassurance, then they have become negatively-reinforcing reassurance.

Educating your client that panic attacks never cause death can be useful. I explain to clients that a panic attack will not cause a heart attack if they have had a stress test that has turned out normal. When someone has a heart condition that can lead to a heart attack, a panic attack may trigger the heart attack, but the individual would have had that heart attack soon anyway. The panic is not the cause. For a script of what I tell clients in this situation refer back to the interoceptive exposure section of Chapter 10. While a medical event can be a factor in triggering panic attacks, medical events are never the sole cause of panic. For example, most people who suffer an actual heart attack don't develop panic attacks.

Similarly, educate clients about fainting. Many clients are fearful of fainting during a panic attack. It is very unlikely that

> **Strategy #81: Education vs. reassurance**

fainting will occur during a panic attack. Because fainting is usually triggered by parasympathetic activation, one is less likely than ever to faint during panic because the opposing sympathetic nervous system is usually activated. The exceptions are blood and needle phobia, and on rare occasions in which a panic attack is triggered by a parasympathetic, also called vasovagal, response that can be caused by standing for long periods of time, heat, or exhaustion. Vasovagal syncope is rare and even more rare when unassociated with the aforementioned situations. In such cases, I recommend involving a physician to explore a medical reason for the vasovagal response. Regardless of the cause of the syncope, stimulants, even caffeine, can help to prevent the response. Tensing one's muscles can also help to prevent fainting. However, do *not* suggest this for clients unless you are relatively certain that they are having vasovagal episodes. Clients may unnecessarily drink caffeine and tense their muscles, which can become negatively reinforcing or even exacerbate anxiety.

Remember that cognitive therapy is only useful if the client believes the positive statement to be true. Obviously if attempts to neutralize fears are unsuccessful and lead back to the obsessive hypochondriacal thought, cognitive therapy is not working and the thought becomes a compulsion. Sometimes, it is helpful to have the client recognize that they have had the fear multiple times in the past and the outcome has never occurred. For example, I have had this chest pain at least fifty times before and I have been fine. Self-monitoring by using the worry outcome log (Chapter 4) is a similar strategy that may help the client to experience fearing the negative outcome and then finding that it didn't happen. Another cognitive strategy is to identify the symptom and/ or the fear as panic. For example, the client can say or think "I am physically fine. The fear I'm experiencing is due to my panic disorder and the anxiety sensitivity I have developed."

If clients are unsuccessful with stopping their checking behaviors, introduce "sitting with the urge" to check or postpone the urge

> **Strategy #82: Sitting with the urge to check.**

to check. This is a way to practice mindful acceptance of urges as well as practice in riding out the urge. Begin by asking clients to close their eyes and remain completely still while you time this exercise for three minutes. Below is an example of a script for this:

> *Closing your eyes. Don't move or talk. You can breathe and swallow, otherwise keep completely still.* (If they move, start over). *Noticing any urges you have to move, talk, clear your throat, or otherwise break your silence and stillness. Noticing where you feel any urges that you have. Resist pushing the urges away and making no effort to make them stay, but keep completely still* (pause). *Allowing the urges to be there* (pause) *and just observing your urges. Noticing where the urges are located* (stop for about a minute). *Noticing how the urges you feel now are similar to the urges you have when you want to check your heartbeat.* (pause) *Continuing to observe and accept these urges even though they may be uncomfortable. Feeling the urges, but keeping still* (stop for about another minute). *Noticing if any new urges have arisen and noticing the original urges as well. Continuing to observe and accept any urges.*

After three minutes, tell them that they may open their eyes and move around. Debrief your client. Ask them what the first urges were and what they experienced. Most clients report that their initial urges decreased or disappeared. When they don't, practicing having urges without giving into them can still be helpful.

Similar to sitting with the urge, one can postpone the compulsion. When they feel the urge they are to look at the time and tell themselves that they are not going to check, but that if they feel a need to check five min-

> Strategy #83:
> Understanding the desire to negatively reinforce anxiety.

utes later, they can either check or postpone checking another five minutes. Both of these strategies can be helpful if just trying to resist urges is unsuccessful. "Urge-surfing" in the addiction literature is similar. It involves accepting the urge and waiting for the urge to decrease rather than giving into it and using.

While there are exceptions to the rule, discourage visits to the emergency room and urgent care when people are having panic attacks. This is the ultimate reassurance seeking. If your client develops pain and symptoms that are not explained by panic attacks, of course, it will be good for them to visit urgent care or the ER. Just because your client has panic attacks, it doesn't prevent them from experiencing a true medical emergency. However, if they have the same worries, or they are relatively certain that they are having a panic attack, they shouldn't go to the ER no matter how severe the panic.

When clients repeatedly worry about various physical symptoms, use a problem-solving approach to seeking medical care. Worrying about a physical symptom isn't going to help unless it is evaluated. That leaves the following options: 1) go to the ER or urgent care, 2) make an appointment with a doctor, 3) postpone the decision to a specific time (e.g., "I'll re-evaluate tomorrow morning") or specific event (e.g., if it gets worse). The postponing can go on indefinitely, from postponing several hours to postponing several days.

Again, going to the internet for solutions is not a good option. If clients continue to overuse ERs, physician visits, and the internet for explanations and moderation of their symptoms, it is a good idea to contact the individual's physician or physicians. Enlighten them about the effects of negative reinforcement and discuss a plan to manage their patient's health without negatively reinforcing their fears. It is also a good idea to learn if there are any contraindications to IE and ways that you may help to support the client's medical issues without negatively reinforcing them. That is, are there health care suggestions the doctor has that may help manage symptoms such that you can help with healthy adherence to these suggestions (e.g., an individual with high blood pressure might check their blood pressure more than ten times/ day when their physician only wants them to check it weekly).

IE is invaluable in the treatment of hypochondriacal panic attacks (See Chapter 10). Simply use IE to bring on the symptoms that they fear. Also, verbally flooding the thoughts about abandoning their children, dying, or suffering is usually very effective (See Chapter 10). Sometimes the best way to keep clients from self-reassurance is to flood the fear.

To illustrate how to use these strategies with someone with hypochondriasis, let's use a case example we will call Kyle. Kyle has panic attacks that include chest pain and tachycardia. He has seen his physician who did an EKG and ordered a stress test both indicating a healthy heart. Kyle still felt insecure about his heart so he followed up with a cardiologist who unsuccessfully tried to reassure him that his heart is healthy and that he is just having panic attacks. Kyle feels his carotid artery regularly to feel how fast his heart is beating and to check that it is consistent. Prior to panic attacks he had run about three miles, four or five times a week and now he completely avoids exercise. He "ping-pongs" between fearful thoughts (e.g., What if the doctors missed something and there is something seriously wrong with my heart?) and reassuring thoughts (e.g., My heart is healthy). Although he knows on an intellectual level that his heart is fine, when he has panic attacks he believes that there is something wrong so he considers getting an opinion from another cardiologist. He also has been avoiding caffeine.

The treatment plan for Kyle includes: 1) IE, including getting back to his exercise

Strategy #84: Exercise

routine, 2) avoid reassurance, including self-reassurance and not scheduling with another cardiologist, 3) flood his fearful thoughts that he is going to have a heart attack and the fear that the doctors missed something, 4) stop the habit of checking his carotid artery or otherwise checking his heart, and 5) start using caffeine.

Because Kyle is athletic I would begin by asking him to work up to his old routine of running three miles. Perhaps start with rapid walking or a slow jog until his anxiety reduces or he is worn out. Similarly, in session I'd likely begin with running up two flights of stairs for IE. Emphasize not checking his carotid during these exercises, as well as in between exercises. Similarly, avoid self-reassurance during the exercise. If he is unable to avoid reassurance, he may need to flood his fears during the exercise. This can be done in his mind. However, it might be best to make a recording that he could listen to during his run. Finally, repeating the word "heart attack," either by mumbling quietly as he runs, thinking it in his mind, or using a loop with an app or recording. A script of flooding the feared thought for Kyle is as follows:

> *What if there is something wrong with my heart. What if I have a heart attack and die. What if the doctors missed something. What if the doctors are wrong and that this isn't panic, but a heart defect that hasn't been detected by the tests they have run.*

It is common with clients like Kyle to stop worrying about the health disaster that they have faced and flooded, only to come up with a new hypochondriacal fear. This can happen more than once. So, for instance, let's say that Kyle begins to no longer fear cardiac symptoms and no longer obsesses about a heart defect, only to begin to fear that there is something wrong with his brain due to feeling derealized. He's afraid that he has brain cancer. After flooding this fear and doing IE to induce derealization, he becomes fearful that he will have a pulmonary embolism. In these cases, I have them flood the specific fear, as well as the general fear. That is, flood the current concern as well as the concern that they will "become incapacitated or die as a result of a medical catastrophe." If Kyle had stopped fearing heart attacks, but developed a fear of having a pulmonary embolism an example of a flooding script is as follows:

> *I'm afraid that I will get a pulmonary embolism and die. What if I have something else wrong with my body that will lead to a medical emergency. What if that medical issue causes me to be incapacitated or die. I'm afraid I'll have a pulmonary embolism or another serious medical event causing me to be incapacitated or die.*

To summarize, individuals suffering from hypochondriasis are usually in a habit of negatively reinforcing their fears about medical illness. Helping clients to break this habit includes resisting the urge to engage in avoidance behaviors and facing the fears. "Sitting with the urge" and postponing the avoidance behaviors can be helpful. Facing the fears with verbal flooding and IE are usually necessary in order to overcome the fear of disease and the feared consequences of disease. Education and cognitive therapy can be helpful with hypochondriasis, particularly when clients fear that panic attacks will trigger a medical emergency. However, be careful that these efforts do not result in negatively reinforcing the fears.

CHAPTER FIFTEEN

When CBT Isn't Enough

While CBT is generally very effective in the treatment of worry and panic, some clients' responses to therapy are disappointing. This section presents alternative treatment approaches.

THE EFFECT OF THE 21ST CENTURY ON ANXIETY

Modern society plays an important role in the reasons that so many people suffer from anxiety disorders. Our ancestors' habits were much different than ours. They moved much more, and they were in the sun much more. The stressors they faced were more often physical in nature, while ours are much more likely to be psychological. Regardless of your age, your grandparents probably moved around much more in their daily lives. Their activities of daily living, forms of recreation and, often, their work, required more physical activity. The differences are more marked when we compare ourselves to how people lived centuries ago and even more so thousands of years ago.

Our bodies and minds cannot differentiate between physical threat and psychological threat. As covered in Chapter 5, regardless of whether the threat is a deadline or a bear ready to attack, our sympathetic nervous system gears up to fight or run. Today, most of the time, our sympathetic nervous systems are activated, and the ensuing physiological responses prepare us to fight and run when there is nothing to physically fight and no place to go. The same responses protected our ancestors by helping them to escape danger. Today they are almost always useless and sometimes are harmful. High levels of cardiovascular reactivity – increases in heart rate and blood pressure in response to stress – are predictive of coronary heart disease, hypertension, and the extent of atherosclerotic lesions (Krantz, Contrada, Hill, & Friedler, 1988) and anxiety is associated with a range of health problems (Newman, 2000).

Our ancestors were only privy to tragedy in their own communities and neighboring communities. Today, we are faced with tragedies that occur around the globe. Furthermore, tragedies have become more common with the increasingly deadly bombs and weapons. The psychological weight of these worldwide tragedies certainly affects most of us at least some of the time. It's difficult to see tragedies such as the Sandy Hook Elementary School shooting or the tsunami in Japan without feeling something.

Consider, too, the technological advances of which we try to stay abreast. This can be overwhelming particularly for individuals who didn't grow up with computers, smart phones, and tablets. Because of technology and machines, more people work at their desks and fewer people have jobs that require significant physical activity. Recreational activities have become increasingly sedentary as people choose to play video games and text, rather than getting together for a game of horseshoes or a swim, for example. Exercise stimulates serotonin, norepinephrine, and dopamine, a lack of which are associated with depression and anxiety. In fact, some studies show that moderate exercise (walking or jogging three times per week) is superior to, or as useful as, selective serotonergic reuptake inhibitors (SSRIs) in treating depression (Blumenthal et al., 1999). Exercise can also be helpful for many individuals with anxiety (Asmundson et al., 2013).

As a result of being inside so much more than our ancestors, we don't get enough sunshine and thereby, vitamin D. When we do

> **Strategy #85: Rule out Vitamin D deficiency**

venture into the sun, we often have on so much sunscreen that we block 99% of vitamin D. A lack of vitamin D contributes significantly to anxiety and depression. In addition, stress depletes vitamin D receptors. Forrest and Stuhldreher (2010) reported the results from The National Health and Nutrition Examination Survey, which analyzed data for vitamin D levels in 4,495 adults between 2005 and 2006. Using a very low threshold of =20 ng/mL the overall prevalence rate of vitamin D deficiency was 41.6%, with the highest rate seen in African-Americans (82.1%), followed by Hispanics (69.2%). Bischoff-Ferrari, Giovannucci, Willett, Dietrich, & Dawson-Hughes (2006) reviewed many studies and concluded that vitamin D should be at least 35 to 40 ng/mL. Gilsanz, Kremer, Mo, Tishya and Wren (2010), found 59% of a sample of 90 women to have blood concentrations of less than 30 ng/mL. Naturopaths, and many physicians, recommend a blood level of at least 50 ng/mL. According to that standard, it is likely that well over half of Americans are Vitamin D deficient. The further away from the equator one lives, the greater the risk of Vitamin D deficiency, particularly in winter.

In summary, to address the 21st century's effect on anxiety, decide whether it is healthy for your client to limit their exposure to news. Educate your clients about the benefits of exercise, and encourage them to exercise regularly. Suggest that your clients get tested for Vitamin D deficiency. Be mindful that some labs consider 20 ng/mL to be normal, while many practitioners recommend levels of above 50 ng/mL. Although Vitamin D is readily available without a prescription, it's best to get physician approval regarding supplementation.

PERSONALITY FACTORS ASSOCIATED WITH POOR OUTCOMES IN GAD

As previously mentioned, applied relaxation, self-control desensitization, and cognitive therapy combined with early detection of spirals have been shown to be effective in the treatment of anxiety. These CBT techniques are the only empirically-proven effective treatments for GAD, helping many clients to enjoy high end-state functioning. Despite this fact, CBT leads to a smaller percentage of clients with GAD achieving high end-state functioning than those with other anxiety disorders (Brown, Barlow, & Liebowitz, 1994).

Two characteristics have been associated with poor outcomes: interpersonal issues and emotional avoidance. Clients who scored high on dominant/hostile, intrusive/needy, and vindictive/self-centered on the *Inventory of Interpersonal Problems Circumplex Scales* (Alden, Wiggins, & Pincus, 1990) had significantly poorer response to therapy than those who scored in the normal range. Furthermore, those suffering interpersonal problems at the end of treatment were less likely to maintain their gains at the two-year follow-up (Borkovec et al., 2002). This is not surprising given that the most common comorbid diagnosis amongst clients with GAD is social anxiety disorder.

Clients with GAD are likely to utilize their worries to avoid emotional experience. "I intellectualize to the point I don't have to feel things," illustrates the process that occurs for many GAD sufferers. Borkovec and Roemer (1995) reported that college students meeting criteria for GAD were significantly more likely to endorse the item: "Worrying about most of the things I worry about is a way to distract myself from worrying about even more emotional things, things that I don't want to think about." It follows that individuals who utilize worry as a way to avoid experiencing uncomfortable emotions would find it especially difficult to relinquish worry. They likely fear that if they significantly reduce worrying, uncomfortable feelings may overwhelm them.

People with GAD also feel more threatened by, and perceive greater discomfort from, emotions compared to non-anxious controls (Llera & Newman, 2010). Furthermore, their attempts to control emotion are not only unsuccessful, they may actually lead to hyper-vigilance and more labile emotions (Newman, Castonguay, Borkovec, & Molnar, 2004).

It also seems that once clients process their emotions, they may feel some relief from anxiety. Moreover, depressed clients who experienced more emotions during the course of therapy fared better with CBT than those who did not emote as much (Castonguay, Goldfried, Wiser, Raue, & Hayes, 1996). Although this study involved depressed clients, there is a great deal of comorbidity and overlap in the symptoms of GAD and those of depression. Therefore, these findings are likely generalizable to CBT and anxiety.

For a more extensive review of the literature indicating that interpersonal problems and avoidance of emotional processing prevent CBT from being successful in treating GAD, please see Newman et al. (2011). They review the literature in the introduction of their study comparing CBT with supportive listening and CBT with emotion-focused and interpersonal therapies aimed at improving outcomes with CBT. In the latter group, they used Safran and Segal's (1990) model of interpersonal schema therapy which addresses both interpersonal and emotional issues and combined it with CBT. While both groups were significantly improved, unfortunately there were no statistically significant differences on any of the variables tested. However, results did favor the group that addressed emotional processing and interpersonal problems with 75% of them no longer meeting criteria for GAD at the two-year follow-up compared to 63.6% in the group that received reflective listening.

Although this study was not successful in creating a better outcome by adding a component to address interpersonal issues and avoidance of emotional processing, it is

> Strategy #86: Engage in therapies that promote emotional processing.

recommended that clinicians be mindful of these issues. Directly treat social anxiety and consider utilizing interpersonal psychotherapy to treat the interpersonal deficits. Similarly, I encourage all clinicians to use whatever skills they know to process emotions including, but not limited to, reparenting in schema therapy (Young, Klosko, & Weishaar, 2006) experiential therapies, movement therapy, diaries aimed at recording emotional experience, or other techniques that you may use to help clients emote. Even reflective listening has been shown to lead to significantly higher levels of emotional processing than CBT alone (Borkovec & Costello, 1993) and this may explain why Newman et al., didn't find a greater difference between the groups that received supportive therapy and emotion-focused/interpersonal therapies.

I regularly utilize reparenting as in schema therapy particularly when clients are either unresponsive to CBT or when a life trap such as unrelenting standards (See Chapter 11 on perfectionism) or subjugation (See Chapter 12 on people-pleasing) is obvious. Reparenting involves getting the client relaxed, guiding them through imagery of their childhood home, school, important figures in their lives, etc., and then having them imagine a painful event. When trauma is severe, it may be best to ask them to imagine only the moments after the event. Then I say "imagine that I'm there" and then support them by saying what you think would have been most helpful at the time. Next, have them imagine that they are simultaneously their current self and their child (or younger self) visualizing, imagining, the words and actions (e.g., hug) they wanted at the time. While this strategy is not foolproof, I have seen numerous clients cry or get angry during a reparenting session. As a result of these sessions, clients often enjoy an immediate significant reduction in anxiety the next week. Sometimes the results are amazing such that clients' behaviors change (e.g., people pleasers put themselves first, perfectionists stop working after work) with little or no effort.

Given that mindfulness and relaxation strategies require concentration and that the symptoms of attention deficit hyperactivity disorder (ADHD) are known to cause anxiety and irritability, it follows that having ADHD might interfere with treatment of GAD and panic. In my clinical experience, ADHD rates are relatively high among those with GAD and are not uncommon in panic disorder. I believe that a lack of both adherence and concentration due to ADHD interfere with GAD treatment. Unfortunately, the aforementioned comorbidity studies with GAD used the Anxiety Disorders Interview Schedule-Revised (ADIS-R; DiNardo & Barlow, 1988) to assess for comorbid disorders, and it does not include an assessment of adult ADHD. In children and adolescents with ADHD, 15% were diagnosed with GAD. Comorbidity of adult ADHD and GAD is a suggested topic of research. In the interim, be mindful of assessing and treating co-morbid ADHD in clients with anxiety.

MEDICATION

Many therapists, in my opinion, are too quick to refer to psychiatry for medication to treat GAD and panic attacks. The techniques in this book are much more effective than medication in treating panic according to at least three meta-analyses (Clum et al., 1993; Gould et al., 1993, Westen & Morris, 2001). And an extensive review indicates that CBT is the only effective treatment for GAD (Brown et al., 1994). In addition, other medical causes (e.g., thyroid imbalance, estrogen deficiency) should be ruled out before medicating with anti-depressants or benzodiazepines. Likewise, these problems should be ruled out when choosing therapy alone. Be particularly mindful of hormonal influences in postpartum and peri-menopausal women and in middle-aged men. Given that very few psychologists have prescribing privileges, it is usually necessary to confer with psychiatrists and other prescribing physicians when attempting to enact the suggestions that follow.

Medication certainly has its place in treating anxiety. While CBT is most effective for the majority of clients, there are undeniable individual differences. Some clients respond much better to medication than to CBT even when adherence to CBT strategies is very good. The reasons for referring to a physician to prescribe medication are as follows: therapy is ineffective, poor adherence to CBT between sessions, or the client is unwilling to continue therapy.

Serotonin-selective reuptake inhibitors (SSRIs) are used, but with little success, in treating GAD. There are some outliers who do benefit from SSRIs, and they may be indicated if comorbid depression is present. The use of SSRIs for panic have been shown to be somewhat effective in the treatment of panic attacks and certainly more effective in treating panic than GAD. In some cases SSRIs completely stop panic attacks with few or no side effects. However, sometimes the side effects mimic the symptoms of panic and exacerbate the problem. Physicians and clients alike may be in a hurry to arrive at a therapeutic dose, but a slow titration will be less likely to cause side effects that may actually trigger panic attacks.

Benzodiazepines have been used in treating GAD with little to no success. Studies range from a 40% reduction in GAD with transient results to being no more effective than a placebo (See Brown et al, 1994). Certainly, benzodiazepines will lead to a feeling of being more calm, but do nothing to fundamentally change the habit of worry.

Benzodiazepines, especially Xanax, are frequently used to treat panic attacks. See Chapter 8 for an explanation of how benzodiazepines can negatively reinforce anxiety and how it interferes with exposure therapy. If such medication is desired because the client is unresponsive to therapy, refuses therapy, is unresponsive to SSRIs, or is already dependent upon a benzodiazepine, I recommend one of three medication options: beta-blockers, longer-acting, slower-onset benzodiazepines, or consistent dosing of other benzodiazepines versus as needed use.

Beta-blockers are indicated if the client is having heart-focused panic. Palpitations, the perception that one's heart is racing, appear to be the most common symptom of a panic attack (Barlow et al., 1985). Moreover, clients report them to be more severe than any of the other panic symptoms (Barlow et al., 1985). Beta-blockers are very effective in preventing tachycardia (heart rate of over 100 beats per minute at rest) and slowing the heart rate. Beta-blockers are not addictive and do not negatively reinforce anxiety because they prevent it versus quickly permitting an escape from intense anxiety. They are particularly useful for performance anxiety, including social anxiety, and other situational anxiety (e.g., flying phobia). Therefore, if your client's first symptom or worst symptom is cardiac related, beta-blockers may be very helpful. They are contraindicated if the client has low blood pressure or if the client is experiencing light-headedness with their panic attacks, as beta-blockers can cause light-headedness.

If beta-blockers are taken consistently, they can cause depression, known as the "beta-blocker blues." They may also cause weight gain. If used relatively infrequently on an as-needed basis, these problems are unlikely to occur. Also, if a client is suffering from depression that is secondary to panic, a beta-blocker may lift depression.

If you think beta-blockers may be indicated and make a referral to the physician, it is important for you to discuss this with the physician before your client is evaluated. Otherwise they may prescribe Xanax or another benzodiazepine. To prevent this it may be necessary to explain your concern regarding negative-reinforcement to the physician and why you would like for them to consider a beta-blocker instead.

I recommend against benzodiazepines most of the time. However, if all other treatments have failed, and a client is unable to go to work or school due to an incapacitating fear of panic attacks, longer-acting medications such as Klonipin or Xanax XR (extended release) may be indicated. Similarly, such medications may be chosen in the short term due to immediacy of need to go to school or work. Nonetheless, keep in mind that sometimes acceptance, education, and IE can work very well such that two to three sessions scheduled in a week could effectively reduce panic and prevent dependence on benzo-diazepines. Of course, clients can choose to continue on the longer-acting benzodiazepines if they are well tolerated with few side-effects, but keep in mind that there are side-effects including cognitive deficits that are likely with long-term use.

When a scheduled dose of a long-acting benzodiazepine is used two to three times per day, instead of as-needed, the negative-reinforcement cycle that leads to exacerbation of panic is less likely to occur. This is because longer-acting medications are more likely to prevent symptoms instead of being used to escape symptoms. Faster-acting benzodiazepines with shorter half-lives (e.g., Xanax) create a larger risk of negative reinforcement even when scheduled. However, another option is to consistently dose shorter-acting benzodiazepines. This is not recommended because the rapid onset leads to negative reinforcement, however, some clients are unwilling to switch to a different medication, and arriving at a similar dose with a longer-acting medication can be tricky. Consistent dosing must be very specific (e.g., upon awakening, lunch, dinner, before bed) otherwise clients will be tempted to take doses early if they are anxious, thereby negatively reinforcing anxiety.

For individuals dependent upon benzodiazepines, 76% were able to discontinue when combining a slow taper program with CBT compared to only 24% tapering without CBT. However at the three-month follow-up only 58% of those in the CBT program remained drug-free (Otto et al., 1993). *Stopping Anxiety Medication: Therapist Guide* (Otto & Pollack, 2009) which has an accompanying workbook for clients (Otto & Pollack, 2009) are excellent resources that can be shared with physicians to improve successful benzodiazepine taper and ultimate discontinuation.

Afterword: When CBT Is Not Enough

CBT, designed to treat anxiety, worry, and panic is usually effective. You have learned several traditional CBT strategies as well as many creative new strategies that will help you to provide relief for your anxious clients. In summary, catching anxiety spirals early and using active relaxation throughout the day are particularly helpful in the treatment of worry. While these strategies may be helpful in treating panic, exposure therapies, especially interoceptive exposure, are often more effective than coping strategies (See the decision tree at the end of Chapter 10). Finally, observation and acceptance of anxious thoughts and feelings can be particularly useful for some clients suffering from GAD as well as panic.

When CBT proves ineffective, one can use the approaches covered in this chapter and consider referral to other practitioners for medication, transcranial magnetic stimulation, naturopathy, holistic medicine, chiropractic, or another psychotherapist who may be able to more effectively address the social and emotional issues discussed in this book.

References

Abel, J. L., & Borkovec, T. D. (1995). Generalizability of DSM-III-R generalized anxiety disorder to proposed DSM-IV criteria and cross-validation of proposed changes. *Journal of Anxiety Disorders, 9(4),* 303-313.

Abel, J. L. (2010). *Active relaxation: How to increase productivity and achieve balance by decreasing stress and anxiety.* La Vergne, TN: Lightning Source.

American Psychiatric Association. (2013). Diagnostic and statistical manual of mental disorders (5th ed.).

Andrews, V. H., & Borkovec, T. D. (1988). The differential effects of induction of worry, somatic anxiety, and depression on emotional experience. *Journal of Behavior Therapy and Experimental Psychiatry, 19,* 21-26.

Antony, M. M. & Swinson, R. P. (2000). *Phobic disorders and panic in adults: A guide to assessment and treatment.* Washington, DC: American Psychological Association.,

Asmundson, J. G., Fetzner, M. G., DeBoer, L. B., Powers, M. B., Otto, M. W., & Smits, A. J. (2013). Let's get physical: A contemporary review of the anxiolytic effects of exercise for anxiety and its disorders. *Depression and Anxiety, 30(4),* 362-73.

Barlow, D. H., Vermilyea, J., Blanchard, E. B. Vermilyea, B. B., Di Nardo, P. A. & Cerny, J. A. (1985). The phenomenon of panic. *Journal of Abnormal Psychology, 94(3),* 320-328.

Beck, A.T. (1967). *The diagnosis and management of depression.* Philadelphia, PA: University of Pennsylvania Press.

Beck, A. T., Sokol, L., Clark, D. M., Berchick, B., & Wright, F. (1992). A cross-over study of focused cognitive therapy for panic disorder. *American Journal of Psychiatry, 149,* 778–783.

Behar, E., & Borkovec, T. D. (2002, November). *Cognitive-behavioral therapy for generalized anxiety disorder: Changes in dysfunctional attitudes.* Poster presented at the 35th Annual Association for the Advancement of Behavior Therapy, Reno, NV.

Bernstein, D. A. & Borkovec, T. D. (1973). *Progressive relaxation training: A manual for the helping profession.* Champaign, IL: Research Press.

Bernstein, D.A., Borkovec, T.D., & Hazlett-Stevens, H. (2000). *New directions in progressive relaxation training: A guidebook for helping professionals.* Westport, CT: Praeger Publishers.

Bischoff-Ferrari, H. A., Giovannucci, E., Willett, W. C. Dietrich, T. & Dawson-Hughes, B. (2006). Estimation of optimal serum concentrations of 25-hydroxyvitamin D for multiple health outcomes. *American Journal of Clinical Nutrition, 84(1),* 18-28.

Blatt, S. B., Quinlan, D. M. Pilkonis, P.A., & Shea, M. T. (1995). The destructiveness of perfectionism: Implications for the treatment of depression. *Journal of Consulting and Clinical Psychology, 63,* 125-132

Blumenthal, J. A., Babyak, M. A., Moore, K. A., Craighead, W. E., Herman S., Khatri P., et al. (1999). Effects of exercise training on older patients with major depression. *Archives of Internal Medicine, 159(19),* 2349-56

Borkovec, T. D. & Costello E. (1993). Efficacy of applied relaxation and cognitive-behavioral therapy in the treatment of generalized anxiety disorder. *Journal of Consulting and Clinical Psychology, 61(4),* 611-619.

Borkovec, T. D., Abel, J. L., & Newman H. (1995). Effects of comorbid conditions in generalized anxiety disorder. *Journal of Consulting and Clinical Psychology, 63(3),* 479-483.

Borkovec, T. D., Newman, M. G., Pincus, A. L. & Lytle, R. (2002). A component analysis of cognitive-behavioral therapy for generalized anxiety disorder and the role of interpersonal problems. *Journal of Consulting and Clinical Psychology, 70(2),* 288-298.

Borkovec, T. D., & Sharpless, B. (2004). Generalized anxiety disorder: Bringing cognitive behavioral therapy into the valued present. In S. Hayes, V. Follette, & M. Linehan (Eds.), *New directions in behavior therapy,* (pp. 209-242). New York: Guilford Press.

Brown, T. A., & Barlow, D. H. (1992). Comorbidity among anxiety disorders: Implications for treatment and DSM-IV. *Journal of Consulting and Clinical Psychology, 60,* 835-844.

Brown, T. A., Barlow, D. H., & Liebowitz, M. R. (1994). The empirical basis of generalized anxiety disorder. *American Journal of Psychiatry, 151,* 1272-1280.

Burns, D. D. (1980). *Feeling good: The new mood therapy.* New York: Wm. Morrow and Co.

Castonguay, L. G., Goldfried, M. R., Wiser, S., Raue, P. J., & Hayes, A. M. (1996). Predicting the effect of cognitive therapy for depression: A study of unique and common factors. *Journal of Consulting and Clinical Psychology, 64,* 497-504.

Clum, G. A., Clum, G., & Surls, R. A. (1993). A meta-analysis of treatments for panic disorder. *Journal of Consulting and Clinical Psychology, 61(2),* 317-326.

Craske, M. G., Brown, T. A., & Barlow, D. H. (1991). Behavioral treatment of panic disorder: A two-year follow-up. *Behavior Therapy, 22(3),* 289-304.

Craske, M.G., and Barlow, D.H. (2006) *Mastery of your anxiety and panic: Workbook: Treatments that work.* Oxford University Press. Oxford, UK.

da Silva, P., & Rachmann, S. (1984). Does escape behavior strengthen agoraphobic avoidance? A preliminary study. *Behaviour Research and Therapy, 11,* 87-91.

Dugas, M. J., Letarte, H., Rhéaume, J., Freeston, M., & Ladouceurr R. (1995). worry and problem solving: Evidence of a specific relationship. *Cognitive Therapy and Research. 19(1),* 109-120.

DiNardo, P. A,, & Barlow, D. H. (1988). Anxiety Disorders Interview Schedule—Revised (ADIS-R). Albany: State University of New York, Phobia and Anxiety Disorder Clinic.

Eifert, G. H., & Heffner, M. (2003). The effects of acceptance versus control contexts on avoidance of panic-related symptoms. *Journal of Behavior Therapy and Experimental Psychiatry, 34,* 293-312.

Ellis, A. 1975. *A new guide to rational living.* Upper Saddle River, N.J.: Prentice-Hall.

Epstein, M. 1998. Going to pieces without falling apart: A buddhist's perspective on wholeness. New York,: Broadway Books.

Forrest, K.Y., & Stuhldreher WL. (2011). Prevalence and correlates of vitamin D deficiency in US adults. *Nutrition Research, 31*(1), 48-54.

Garssen, B., Buikhuisen, M. & vanDyke, R. (1996). Hyperventilation and panic attacks. *American Journal of Psychiatry, 153,* 513-518.

Geffen, D.(Producer) & Oz, F. (Director). (1986). *Little shop of horrors*[Motion picture]. United States: The Geffen Company.

Gilsanz, V., Kremer, A., Mo A.O., Wren, T. A. & Kremer, R. (2010). Vitamin D status and its relation to muscle mass and muscle fat in young women. *Journal of Clinical Endocrinology & Metabolism, 95(4),*1595-60.

Gould, R.A., Otto, M. W. & Pollack, M.H. (1993). A meta-analysis of treatment outcome for panic disorder. *American Journal of Psychiatry, 150(10),* 1485-90.

Hayes, S. C., Smith, S (2005). *Get out of your mind and into your life: The new acceptance and commitment therapy.* Oakland, CA: New Harbinger Publications.

Hayes, S. C., Strosahl, K.D., Wilson, K.G., & Strosahl, K.D. (2011). *Acceptance and commitment therapy,: The process and practice of mindful change* (2nd ed.). New York: Guilford Press.

Hazlette-Stevens, H. (2005). Women who worry too much: how to stop worry & anxiety from ruining relationships, work, & fun. Oakland, C.A.: New Harbinger Publications.

Houston, P. 2000. A *little more about me.* New York: Washington Square Press.

Jakubowski, P., & Lange, A.J. (1978). The assertive option: Your rights and responsibilities. Champaign, IL: Research Press

Kabat-Zinn, J. 1990. Full catastrophe living: *Using the wisdom of your body and mind to face stress, pain, and illness.* New York: Random House,

Krantz, D. S., Contrada, R. J., Hill, D. R., & Friedler, E. (1988). Environmental stress and biobehavioral antecedents of coronary heart disease. *Journal of Consulting and Clinical Psychology, 56,* 331-341.

Lee S., Wu J., Ma Y.L., Tsang A., Guo W. J.,& Sung J. (2009). Irritable bowel syndrome is strongly associated with generalized anxiety disorder: a community study. *Alimentary Pharmacology & Therapeutics Journal, 15;30(6):*643-51.

Lindemann (1944). Symptomatology and management of acute grief. *American Journal of Psychiatry*, 101, 141-148.

Linehan, M. M. (1993). Skills training manual for treatment of borderline personality disorder. New York Guilford Press

Llera, S. J., & Newman, M. G. (2010). Effects of worry on physiological and subjective reactivity to emotional stimuli in generalized anxiety disorder and nonanxious control participants. *Emotion, 10,* 640–650.

Mayo Clinic [Internet]. Rochester, MN: 2011, Jan 7 Dehydration; [cited 2013 Aug 17] [about 2 p.] Available from: http://www.mayoclinic.com/health/dehydration/DS00561/DSECTION=symptoms

MedlinePlus [Internet]. Bethesda (MD): National Library of Medicine (US); [updated 2013 Aug 12]. Hypoglycemia; [updated 2013 Aug 12; reviewed 2013 Aug 12; cited 2013 Aug 17]; [about 2 p.]. Available from: http://www.nlm.nih.gov/medlineplus/hypoglycemia.html

Meuret AE, Rosenfield D, Wilhelm FH, Zhou E, Conrad A, Ritz T, & Roth WT. (2011) Do unexpected panic attacks occur spontaneously? *Biological Psychiatry, 70(10),*985-91.

Mitchell, J. H., Newall, C., Broeren, S. & Hudson, J. L. (2013) The role of perfectionism in cognitive behaviour therapy outcomes for clinically anxious children. *Behaviour Research and Therapy 51(9),* 547-554.

Miramax. (2001). Amélie.

Molina, S., Borkovec, T. D., Peasely, C., & Person, D. (1998). Content analysis of worrisome streams of consciousness in anxious and dysphoric participants. *Cognitive Therapy and Research, 22,* 109-123.

Newman, M.G. (2000). Recommendations for a cost offset model of psychotherapy allocation using generalized anxiety disorder as an example. *Journal of Consulting and Clinical Psychology, 68,* 549-555.

Newman, M. G., Castonguay, L. G., Borkovec, T. D., & Molnar, C. (2004). Integrative psychotherapy. In R. G. Heimberg, C. L. Turk, & D. S. Mennin (Eds.), *Generalized anxiety disorder: Advances in research and practice* (pp. 320–350). New York,: Guilford Press.

Newman, M.G., Castonguay, L.G., Borkovec, T.D., Fisher, A.J., Boswell, J.F., Szkodny, L.E. & et al. (2011) A randomized controlled trial of cognitive-behavioral therapy for generalized anxiety disorder with integrated techniques from emotion-focused and interpersonal therapies. *Journal of Consulting and Clinical Psychology, 79(2),* 171–181.

Otto MW , Pollack MH, Sachs GS, Reiter SR, Meltzer-Brody S, Rosenbaum JF. (1993) Discontinuation of benzodiazepine treatment: efficacy of cognitive-behavioral therapy for patients with panic disorder. *American Journal of Psychiatry, 150(10)*1485-90.

Otto, M.W., &Pollack, D.H. (2009). Stopping anxiety medication workbook: Treatments that work. . Oxford, UK: Oxford University Press

Otto, M.W., &Pollack, D.H. (2009). Stopping anxiety medication therapist guide: Treatments that work. Oxford, UK.: Oxford University Press.

Peale, N. V, (1952) *The power of positive thinking.* New York: Simon and Schuster,

Pennebaker, J.W. (1985). Inhibition and cognition: Toward an understanding of trauma and disease. *Canadian Psychology, 26,* 82-95.

Rachman, S., Craske, M.G., Tallman K., & Solyom, C. (1984). Does escape behaviour strengthen agoraphobic avoidance? A replication. *Behavior Therapy, 17,* 366-384.

Ristad, E. 1981. *A soprano on her head: right-side-up reflections on life and other performances.* London: Dorian Press.

Roy-Byrne, P. P. (1996). Generalized anxiety and mixed anxiety-depression: Association with disability and health care utilization. *Journal of Clinical Psychiatry, 57(Suppl 7),* 86-91.

Safran, J. D., & Segal, Z. V. (1990). Interpersonal process in cognitive therapy. New York: Basic Books.

Sawyer, K. R. (2007). *Group Genius.* New York: Basic Books.

Schmidt, N.B., Woolaway-Bickel, K., Trakowski, J.H., Santiago, H.T., Storey, J., Koselka M., Cook, J.(2000). Dismantling cognitive-behavioral treatment for panic disorder: Questioning the utility of breathing retraining. *Journal of Consulting and Clinical Psychology, 68(3):*417-24.

Stern, R. & Marks, I. (1973). Brief and prolonged flooding: A comparison in agoraphobic patients. *Archives of General Psychiatry, 28,* 270-276.

Stuart, G. L., Treat, T. A., Wade, W. A. (2000) Effectiveness of an Empirically Based Treatment for Panic Disorder Delivered in a Service Clinic Setting: 1-Year Follow-Up. *Journal of Consulting and Clinical Psychology. 68(3)* 506-512.

Telch, M. J., Lucas, J. A., Schmidt, N. B., Hanna, H. H., LaNae Jaimez, T., & Lucas, R. A. (1993). Group cognitive-behavioral treatment of panic disorder. *Behaviour Research and Therapy, 31,* 279-87.

Thayer, J. F., Friedman, B. H., & Borkovec, T. D. (1996). Autonomic characteristics of generalized anxiety disorder and worry. Biological Psychiatry, 39, 255-266.

Warner Brothers Pictures. 2001. Harry Potter and the Sorcerer's Stone.

Wegner, D. 1989. *White Bears and Other Unwanted Thoughts*. New York: Guilford Press.

Westen, D., Morrison, K. (2001) A multidimensional meta-analysis of treatments for depression, panic, and generalized anxiety disorder: An empirical examination of the status of empirically supported therapies. *Journal of Consulting and Clinical Psychology. 69(6) 875-899.*

Yerkes, R.M., & Dodson, J.D. (1908) The relation of strength of stimulus to rapidity of habit-formation. *Journal of Comparative Neurology and Psychology, 18,* 459-482.

Young, J.E., & Klosko, J.S. (1994). *Reinventing your life: The breakthrough program to end negative behavior and feel great again.* New York: Plume Publishers.

Young, J.E., Klosko, J.S. Weishaar, M.E. (2006). *Schema therapy: A practitioner's guide.* The Guilford Press.

About the Author

Jennifer L. Abel, Ph.D., has specialized in the cognitive-behavioral treatment of anxiety disorders for over 20 years. Before opening a private practice, she served as the associate director of the Stress and Anxiety Disorders Institute at Pennsylvania State University.

Dr. Abel has published many articles in professional journals on the topic of anxiety and is the author of *Active Relaxation: How to Increase Productivity and Achieve Balance by Decreasing Stress and Anxiety.*